Dale Turner is available for seminars, consulting and answering questions about this book by contacting him at:

dale6@roadrunner.com (preferred)
330-335-0162

Free downloads:

Spiritual Gifts Survey	FRANgelism Form
Spiritual Gifts Defined	TLC Monthly Report
Opportunities for Ministry	Child Care Voucher

At Dale's Website

www.First100Days.mobi

TLC Groups for Busy Disciples

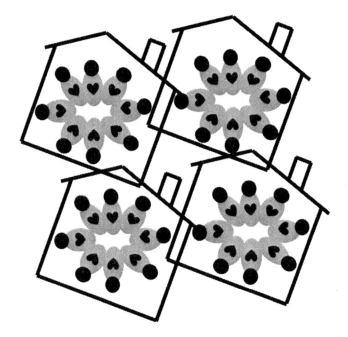

**How to Multiply Groups from
House to House and Grow Your Church!**

by

Dale R. Turner

Dedicated

To: My loving wife Lois whose help and patience made this book possible!

To: My good friends in the Gospel who got me started writing books and doing seminars Rev. Bill Easum and Dr. Stanley Menking,

To: Rev. Don Ebert, lead pastor at Wadsworth United Methodist Church, who trusted me with the process of creating TLC Groups at the Wadsworth Church and who himself became a TLC Pastor.

To: The many great disciples at the Wadsworth church who helped start this experimental ministry.

Content

~ Content ~

Chapter Four – Serving   54-80

Chapter Five – Giving   81-88

Chapter Six – Understanding Scripture   89-105

Content

Chapter Seven – Becoming a TLC Leader 106-110

Chapter Eight – Supplements   111-132

Notes   133-136

Resources for Further Reading   137-138

A Final Word   138

Endorsements   139-140

TLC Groups For Busy Disciples

~ Introduction ~

The Concept

The following is a leadership training and study resource for TLC (Tender Loving Care) groups written by Dale R. Turner for use in local churches. The concept of TLC groups is adapted from the work of Dr. Dale Galloway, former pastor of New Hope Community church in Portland Oregon.[1]

The Biblical Background for Small Groups

For nearly two thousand years Christians have been meeting together in small groups. Jesus brought together a small group of twelve. The early Christians met as a group in the temple, and they had their meals together in their homes, eating with glad and humble hearts. (Acts 2:46 NRSV). The first Methodists led by John Wesley in the 1700's were noted for their weekly small group gatherings called class meetings led by class leaders. A description of those first meetings is given by Dr. David Lowes Watson, "It was therefore agreed that the members of each class should meet together once a week, not only to collect the weekly contributions, but also to give advice, reproof, or encouragement as needed. A dynamic of Christian fellowship quickly developed, as members began to bear one another's burdens, and to care for each other."[2] Christians today are again taking an interest in small groups. Wherever renewal or growth is happening, small groups are involved.

What is a TLC group?

A TLC group is a small group that meets weekly for 59 minutes in a host home for the primary purpose of Christian nurture and growth. The group is led by a TLC pastor trained by the church pastor and staff. The group meets in a host home of church members also trained by the pastor and staff. The group follows a flexible schedule which includes prayer, sharing, lesson discussion, mission and growth. The group is designed for busy 21st century families. The meeting length is kept to 59 minutes (a fun way of saying that it is strictly one hour long). Vouchered expenses for child care are

TLC Groups For Busy Disciples

provided to help families with children participate. The groups are intergenerational and focused on individuals from the youngest infants to the oldest adults. Child care is provided for infants through sixth-graders via vouchered reimbursements and/or a provided list of child care persons. The small group participants range in age from seventh grade through adults.

What Do TLC Groups Actually Do?

The groups study the Bible in relation to its teaching about "the purpose driven life, and the Christian calling to follow Christ by praying, worshipping, giving, serving, and witnessing. Group members support each other with prayers and group discussions. Each group adopts a mission project to reach out to others in the community and/or world. Technically speaking TLC groups are not study groups though they will study the Bible. They are not prayer groups though they will pray. They are not mission groups though they will do mission. They are not therapy groups though they will give support. They are not men's groups, women's groups, singles groups, youth groups, or parents groups, though they will include individuals from all ages and stages of life. The ultimate purpose of the groups is as described, tender loving care.

The Order of a TLC Meeting

The weekly order of a TLC Group is very flexible and will generally include four parts. 1). Get Acquainted Time, 2). Conversational Prayer, 3). Lesson Discussion, and 4). Vision Sharing. However the basic purpose is TLC, so some weeks study may be shorter and prayer longer or vise versa. Some weeks visioning may take more time. Some weeks icebreakers and get-acquainted time may take longer. All depends on how the Holy Spirit is leading and the needs of the group present themselves each week.

Introduction

How to Get Involved in a TLC Group

Contact one of the host families, or one of the TLC pastors, or just show up at one of the host homes listed in the TLC promotional brochure. Groups are designed with growth in mind, so feel free to bring friends with you. When the groups reach an average attendance of 20, they will multiply into two or more groups so they can keep growing. There is always room for more!

TLC in a Nut Shell

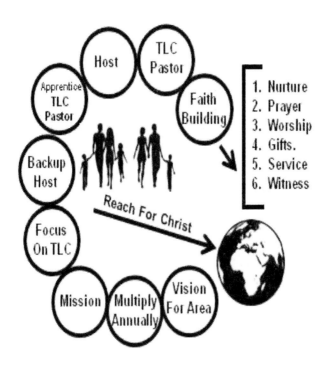

TLC Groups For Busy Disciples

Introduction

TLC Groups For Busy Disciples

32 Week Schedule

Week	Topic	Lesson	Page
	Introduction		
1	The Basic Idea of TLC Groups	1	8-9
2	The TLC Covenant	3	11-12
	Prayer		
3	The Discovery of Conversational Prayer	4	14-15
4	Unanswered Prayer	6	17-19
5	To Whom Should We Pray?	7	19-20
6	For Whom Should We Pray?	8	20-22
7	Five Types of Prayer	9	22-24
	Witness		
8	The Ultimate Walk Across the Room	12	30-31
9	Your Personal Story	14	35-37
10	Your FRANgelism List	15	37-39
11	How to pray With Someone	16	39-41
	Worship		
12	What is Worship?	17	43-45
13	Worship, More Than a Habit	19	47-49
14	Can/Should Worship be Fun?	20	49-51
	Service		
15	The meaning of Spiritual Gifts	22	55-56
16	Discovering Your Spiritual Gifts	23	56-58
17	The Enabling Gifts	24	58-60
18	The Serving Gifts	25	61-62
19	The Other Gifts	26	63-65
20	You Were Made for Mission	29	70-72
21	The Elements of a Mission Statement	30	72-74
22	Writing your personal Mission Statement	31	74-76
23	How Mission Fits With your Spiritual Gifts	32	76-78
	Gifts		
24	Sermon on the Amount	34	82-83
25	Tithes and Offerings	35	84-85
26	Growth in Giving	36	86-88
	Holidays		
27	Thanksgiving Week	n/a	
28	Christmas Week	n/a	
29	New Years Week	n/a	
30	Ash Wednesday Week	n/a	
31	Palm Sunday Week	n/a	
32	Easter Week	n/a	

Introduction

The Basic Idea of TLC Groups - TLC Lesson 1

What is a TLC Group? A TLC group is a small group of people who meet weekly for 59 minutes in a host home for the primary purpose of Christian nurture and growth. The structure of the group has eight components designed for 21st century Christian fellowship and ministry. The eight components are:

1). A TLC Pastor trained by the Pastor and Staff of the church to lead the group.

2). An Apprentice TLC Pastor. A lay person in training preparing to lead a TLC group after the group multiplies.

3). A Host. A lay person or family trained to host the weekly meeting in their home.

4).The general focus of the meeting will be on Tender Loving Care (TLC) or Christian nurture. The group is not designed as a Bible study group, although they will study the Bible. It is not designed as a prayer group, although they will pray, it is not designed as a mission group, although they will do mission, it is not designed as a discussion group, although they will discuss, it is not designed as a support group, although they will be supportive. Help in understanding different types of small groups in churches can be found at the following web site http://www.smallgroups.com/build/models/. Using this site as a guide, TLC groups can be best described as Host groups and/or Cell groups.

5). A group mission will be selected by the group about half way through their annual cycle.

6).The group will multiply annually into two or more groups. The ideal size for a small group is between 6 and 19 people. If necessary the group(s) may need to multiply sooner than 52 weeks, with the recommendation of the Pastor, Staff and TLC Lead Team. (The TLC Lead Team is made up of the Pastors, TLC Pastors and Hosts).

7).Faith building in the form of short weekly topical discussion lessons will be incorporated into the group. Topics are focused on the common Christian practices of Praying, Worshiping, Giving, Serving, and Witnessing. There is no required home work or preparation!

TLC Groups For Busy Disciples

8). Vision for the local area and community will be expressed through individual and group efforts to "Make Disciples of Jesus Christ for The Transformation of The World".

<u>Discussion Questions</u>:

1). What brought you to the TLC group?
2). What questions do you have about TLC groups?

<u>Memory Verse of the Week</u>:

"Day by day, as they spent much time together in the temple, they broke bread at home and ate their food with glad and generous hearts, praising God and having the goodwill of all the people. And day by day the Lord added to their number those who were being saved." (Acts 2:46-47 NRSV).

Ten Characteristics of TLC Groups-TLC Lesson 2

Characteristics differ from components of a TLC Group in that components are the "parts" or "elements" of the group and characteristics are the qualities or things typical of a TLC group. For example one component of the TLC group is that it is lead by a TLC Pastor whereas one characteristic of a TLC group is that it is a close family. Components describe the structure of the group whereas characteristics describe the personality of the group. When we describe the personality of a TLC group we see at least ten things.

1. A close family. Over time people who where once strangers to one another become like a family. "So then, whenever we have an opportunity, let us work for the good of all, and especially for those of the family of faith" (Galatians 6:10 NRSV). "So we, who are many, are one body in Christ, and individually we are members one of another."(Romans 12:5 NRSV).

2). Application of the Bible to daily life. "I have hidden your word in my heart that I might not sin against you." (Psalm 119:11 RSV). Bible reading and memorization.

3). Sharing of life's testimony. "In your hearts reverence Christ as Lord. Always be prepared to make a defense to anyone who calls you to

Introduction

account for the hope that is in you, yet do it with gentleness and reverence."(1. Peter 3:15 RSV).

4). Effective one on one pastoral care. "Is any among you sick? Let him call for the elders of the church, and let them pray over him, anointing him with oil in the name of the Lord; and the prayer of faith will save the sick man, and the Lord will raise him up; and if he has committed sins, he will be forgiven." (James 5:14-15 RSV).

5).Encouragement and edification. "Therefore encourage one another and build one another up, just as you are doing." (I Thessalonians 5:11 RSV).

6). Unlimited opportunities for meaningful service. "For you were called to freedom, brethren; only do not use your freedom as an opportunity for the flesh, but through love be servants of one another." (Galatians 5"13 RSV).

7). Non-threatening friendship evangelism. FRANgelism. "And he said to them, Go into all the world and preach the gospel to the whole creation." (Mark 16:15 RSV).

8). Discipling of new Christians. "For a whole year they met with the church, and taught a large company of people; and in Antioch the disciples were for the first time called Christians." (Acts 11:26 RSV).

9). Spiritual growth. "That Christ may dwell in your hearts through faith; that you, being rooted and grounded in love ... may be filled with all the fullness of God." (Ephesians 3:17-18 RSV).

10).Development of strong leadership. "All scripture is inspired by God and profitable for teaching, for reproof, for correction, and for training in righteousness, that the man of God may be complete, equipped for every good work." (2 Timothy 3:16-17 RSV).

Discussion Question:

1). Which TLC Characteristic most speaks to you right now?

Memory Verse of The Week:
"I have hidden your word in my heart that I might not sin against you." (Psalm 119:11 RSV)

TLC Groups For Busy Disciples

The TLC Covenant - TLC Lesson 3

The dictionary defines a covenant as a contract, pledge, promise, pact, deal or and understanding. In the Bible we have the Old Testament (Covenant) and the New Testament (Covenant). God has made a covenant with God's chosen people numerous times, but the final and lasting covenant is the New Covenant of salvation through Jesus Christ. (John 3:16).

The Covenant is mentioned numerous times in the Old Testament as well as in the New Testament. "He provides food for those who fear him; he is ever mindful of his covenant." (Psalm 111:5 NRSV).

"Then he took a loaf of bread, and when he had given thanks, he broke it and gave it to them, saying, "This is my body, which is given for you. Do this in remembrance of me." And he did the same with the cup after supper, saying, "This cup that is poured out for you is the new covenant in my blood." (Luke 22:19-20 NRSV).

TLC members covenant to:

1). Regularly attend the weekly group meeting.
2). Maintain the confidentiality of all persons in the group.
3). Nurture and support one another in times of need.
4). Maintain accountability to the group for the life of discipleship.
5). Pursue a life of prayer and spiritual growth.
6). Develop a life of personal witness and faith sharing.
7). Support the mission of the group.
8). Train TLC Pastors, Apprentices, Hosts, and Backup Hosts.
9). Multiply the group into two or more groups at the end of the TLC
       year.

Dr. David Lowes Watson describes the early Methodists in the following way, "It was therefore agreed that the members of each class should meet together once a week, not only to collect the weekly contributions, but also to give advice, reproof, or encouragement as needed. A dynamic of Christian fellowship quickly developed, as members began to bear one another's burdens, and to care for each other."[3]

The concept of a TLC covenant is no different than the renewal of our membership vows which we do on membership Sundays when new members join our church. In a sense we have already made such a

Introduction

covenant by joining church. The TLC group is simply a way of supporting our membership covenant in a mutually accountable relationship.

Discussion Questions:

1). What is the easiest part of our group covenant to keep?
2). What is the most difficult part of our group covenant to keep?

Memory Verse of The Week:

"Then he took a loaf of bread, and when he had given thanks, he broke it and gave it to them, saying, "This is my body, which is given for you. Do this in remembrance of me." And he did the same with the cup after supper, saying, "This cup that is poured out for you is the new covenant in my blood." (Luke 22:19-20 NRSV).

TLC Groups for Busy Disciples

~ Chapter One - Praying ~

Chapter One Praying

Discovery of Conversational Prayer-TLC Lesson 4

Rosalind Beatrice Rinker (1906-2002) was born April 2, 1906, in New Rockford, North Dakota. Converted at the age of 15, Rinker sailed to China at the age of 20 to work for the Oriental Mission Society (now OMS International). She served in China for 14 years as a secretary, teacher, and evangelist. As the political climate in China got dangerous, Rinker came back to the U.S. and enrolled at Asbury College in Wilmore, Kentucky. Upon graduating in 1945, she began working as a staff counselor for InterVarsity Christian Fellowship. She worked three years in New York City and eleven years in the Pacific Northwest. Rinker wrote extensively, which resulted in many speaking engagements. Many of these engagements were workshops based on her well-known book, *Prayer: Conversing with God*, which taught Christians about the art of conversational prayer. In October 2006, *Christianity Today Magazine* published its list of "The Top 50 Books That Have Shaped Evangelicals" (over the past 50 years). Rinker's *Prayer: Conversing with God* was voted number one on that list by *CT*'s editors. The magazine had this to say: "In the 1950s, evangelical prayer was characterized by Elizabethan 'wouldsts' and 'shouldsts'. Prayer meetings were often little more than a series of formal prayer speeches. Then Rosalind Rinker taught us something revolutionary: Prayer is a conversation with God. The idea took hold; Today evangelicals assume that casual, colloquial, intimate prayer is the most authentic way to pray."[4]

Rosalind describes her first experience of conversational prayer in these words, "as I remember, Mildred was praying for Ming-lee in a situation that concerned her sister-in-law. Now I'd forgotten to tell Mildred that Ming-lee had sent a little note to me that morning, and that the situation for which Mildred was praying had already been cleared up. Her prayer was already answered and she didn't know it! Without thinking, I interrupted her prayer, and continued it as mine, "We thank Thee, Lord, and that Thou hast already answered that prayer. Ming-lee has already been able to forgive her sister-in-law." I stopped, startled by my own audacity at interrupting Mildred's prayer. There was a moment of silence, and then with great relief both of us sat back and laughed." [5]

Elements of Conversational Prayer.

1. Do not begin with "Prayer Requests", just pray! Someone begins to pray about someone or something in a short sentence or so. (i.e. "Lord, be with Judy as she goes for surgery this week")

TLC Groups for Busy Disciples

2. Someone else jumps in and continues the prayer with another sentence related to the first topic. (i.e."Yes Lord, and give strength to Judy's husband John while she is in the hospital".)

3. Another person jumps in who says, "and take care of John and Judy's children", followed by someone else who says, "and give the doctors wisdom as they do her surgery".

4. The first person jumps in with, "heal Judy Lord", followed by a person who starts a totally different topic, (i.e. "Lord be with our Pastor as she plans for our leadership retreat next week", followed by a series of one line prayers about the retreat,)

5. Stick to the subject.

6, Everyone participates.

7. No one monopolizes.

8. There are no speeches and no fancy language with "Thee's or Thou's".

<u>**Discussion Questions**</u>:

1. How is conversational prayer different from other ways of praying?
2. What might be some of the benefits of Conversational Prayer?

<u>**Memory Verse of The Week**</u>:

"Call to me and I will answer you, and will tell you great and hidden things which you have not known". (Jeremiah 33:3 RSV).

What to Say When You pray - TLC Lesson 5

Many people hesitate to pray because they are not sure what to say. Many more people are afraid to pray out loud in front of others because they fear that they don't have the proper "skills" to use the right words and vocal tones. Others are unsure about whom God is and if God will accept their prayers. The following are some key ideas on how to learn what to say when you pray.

1. Begin with a relationship with the personal God. "And without faith it is impossible to please God, for whoever would approach him must that he exists and that he rewards those who seek him." (Hebrews 11:6 NRSV).

Chapter One Praying

"Some friends play at friendship but a true friend sticks closer than one's nearest kin." (Proverbs 18:24 NRSV). "Let us therefore approach the throne of grace with boldness, so that we may receive mercy and find grace to help in time of need." (Hebrews 4:16 NRSV). "God never uses his love to hurt us. To do so would countermand his own law of judgment. "Do unto others as you would have them do unto you." So he will never let us down, he will never forsake us. His love is extended to all, and he knows exactly how to reach each person."[6]

2. Talk with God as with a Friend. Jesus taught his disciples to be in a close friendship with God. Speak with God as with your father. Talk with respectful closeness. Ask God for daily needs (bread). Confess you sins, (i.e. "I messed up Lord!"). Pray for others. Forgive and be forgiven. "I do not call you servants any longer, because the servant does not know what the master is doing; but I have called you friends, because I have made known to you everything that I have heard from my Father." (John 15:15 NRSV).

Pray like this: 'Our Father in heaven, may your name be kept holy. Let your Kingdom come. Let your will be done, as in heaven, so on earth. Give us today our daily bread. Forgive us our debts, as we also forgive our debtors. Bring us not into temptation, but deliver us from the evil one. For yours are the Kingdom, the power, and the glory forever. Amen. (Matthew 6:9-12 WEB). "When we pray, we're communicating with a real person. We're talking to someone who hears and understands us. God feels the joy, the excitement, the sorrow or the pain we have at that moment. And God knows there are times when we won't know what to say. That's OK. We're permitted to just rest in God, to pray without words. Besides, true friends can be in each other's company without talking".[7]

3. Use everyday language. Use common everyday English, not King James English. Remember that it is not the words we say but the intentions of our hearts that counts. The more natural the prayer, the more real God becomes. Use conversational tones and drop impressive prayer tones and God language. Speak with God as a personal God. Let us learn from King David, who was a true friend of God…**"I have found David the son of Jesse, a man after my own heart, who will do all my will"** (Acts 13:22 RSV).

4. Be Silent and Listen for God to Speak. Listening to God is like listening to anyone, before you can hear God; you must be ready to listen. Just as in a conversation, you cannot hear the other person if you are talking or if your mind is distracted. So it is with God. If you want to hear God speak, you must be quiet and you must be focused on what God is saying. Regular conversation with God can transform your life! Consider

identifying a place and time to meet with God every day. Prayer is how you begin a conversation with God. Think of it as saying "hello."[8] (Adapted from the Webpage "All About God).

Discussion Questions:

1. What do you say when you pray?
2. How have you experienced listening to God?

Memory Verse of the Week:

"There are friends who pretend to be friends, but there is a friend who sticks closer than a brother". (Psalm 18:24 RSV).

Unanswered Prayer - TLC Lesson 6

Most people, even those who deeply believe in prayer, have sometimes wondered why, at times, prayer seems to go unanswered. The fact is, in my opinion, there is no such thing as unanswered prayer! It has been said that "God only gives three answers to prayer, yes, not yet, and I have something better in mind". Author Joyce Meyer once said, "I have learned from personal experience that putting trust in God means there will be some unanswered questions. That was a hard lesson for me because I naturally want to understand everything... to know what's going on so I can feel like I'm in control". Unanswered questions are not the same as unanswered prayers. So how do we deal with God's three answers to prayer?

1. When God Says, "Not Yet".

A). God might have a growth plan in mind for us. "And to keep me from being too elated by the abundance of revelations, a thorn was given me in the flesh, a messenger of Satan, to harass me, to keep me from being too elated. Three times I am sought the Lord about this, that it should leave me; but he said to me, "My grace is sufficient for you, for my power is made perfect in weakness. (The Apostle Paul, 2 Corinthians 12:7-9 RSV)

B). God might have a destiny in mind for us."Father, if thou art willing, remove this cup from me; nevertheless not my will, but thine, be done". (Jesus praying in the garden).

Chapter One Praying

C). God might want us to know that God is in charge. "And the Lord said to Job: "Shall a faultfinder contend with the Almighty? He, who argues with God, let him answer it." (Job 40:1-2 RSV)

2. When God Says, "Yes".

Bob Hostetler said in the September 22, 2015 issue of Guideposts, there are some prayers God can't resist.

A). I surrender. Jesus said, "Whoever come to me I will never cast out". (John 6:37 RSV)

B). Have your way. "Your kingdom come your will be done". (Matthew 6:10 RSV)

C). Forgive me. "If we confess our sins, he is faithful and just, and will forgive our sins and cleanse us from all unrighteousness (1 John 19 RSV)

D). Lead me. "Lead me, O Lord, in thy righteousness because of my enemies; make thy way straight before me". (Psalm 5:8 RSV).

E). Use me. "Go therefore and make disciples of all nations". (Matthew 28:19 RSV)

F). Make me like you. "And we all, with unveiled face, beholding the glory of the Lord, are being changed into his likeness from one degree of glory to another; for this comes from the Lord who is the Spirit. (2 Corinthians 3:18 RSV).

3. When God Says, "I Have Something Better in Mind."

I asked for strength that I might achieve; I was made weak that I might learn humbly to obey. I asked for health that I might do greater things; I was given infirmity that I might do better things. I asked for riches that I might be happy; I was given poverty that I might be wise. I asked for power that I might have the praise of men; I was given weakness that I might feel the need of God. I asked for all things that I might enjoy life; I was given life that I might enjoy all things. I got nothing that I had asked for, but everything that I had hoped for. Almost despite myself my unspoken prayers were answered; I am, among all men, most richly blessed.

From - "The Blessing of Unanswered Prayers", by an unknown Confederate Soldier

Discussion Questions

TLC Groups for Busy Disciples

1. Describe a time when God said not yet to you.
2. Describe a time when God said yes to you.

<u>Memory Verse of the week</u>:

"Ask, and it will be given you; seek, and you will find; knock, and it will be opened to you. (Matthew 7:7 RSV)

To Whom Should We Pray? - TLC Lesson 7

"All prayer should be directed to our triune God—Father, Son, and Holy Spirit. The Bible teaches that we can pray to one or all three, because all three are one. To the Father we pray with the psalmist, "Listen to my cry for helps, my King and my God, for to you I pray" (Psalm 5:2 RSV). To the Lord Jesus, we pray as to the Father because they are equal. Prayer to one member of the Trinity is prayer to all. Stephen, as he was being martyred, prayed, "Lord Jesus, receive my spirit" (Acts 7:59 RSV). We are also to pray in the name of Christ. Paul exhorted the Ephesian believers to always give "thanks to God the Father for everything, in the name of our Lord Jesus Christ" (Ephesians 5:20 RSV). Jesus assured His disciples that whatever they asked in His name—meaning in His will—would be granted (John 15:16; 16:23 RSV). We are told to pray in the Spirit and in His power. The Spirit helps us to pray, even when we do not know how or what to ask for (Romans 8:26 RSV), (Jude 20 RSV). Perhaps the best way to understand the role of the Trinity in prayer is that we pray to the Father, through (or in the name of) the Son, by the power of the Holy Spirit. All three are active participants in the believer's prayer.[9]

"One of the hardest things to understand about Christianity is the doctrine of the Trinity. God is three in one. God is the Father, Son and Holy Spirit. All three are God and each has a distinct personality. The Father is the Creator. The Son is the Savior. The Holy Spirit is the Counselor and Comforter. I like to describe it this way: When I tell you to turn on the light, you go to a switch that sends an electric current through a wire to the bulb. All three—the switch, the wire and the bulb—produce a single light. It is the same with the Father, Son and Holy Spirit. God is one, but three persons. This means that Jesus is God, and there was a time in history when he became a human. After Jesus died on the cross as a sacrifice for our sins, he went back to heaven to reside there. He sent the Holy Spirit, also God, to dwell in every believer to comfort and counsel us. Because all three persons of

Chapter One Praying

the Trinity are God, you can address God in many ways. If you say "Our Father" or "Jesus" or "Holy Spirit," you are talking to God"[1]

Prayer to the Holy Spirit:

"Come, Holy Spirit, fill the hearts of your faithful. And kindle in them the fire of your love. Send forth Your Spirit and they shall be created. And you will renew the face of the earth".[11]

Prayer to Jesus:

"The shortest, simplest, and most powerful prayer in the world is called the "Jesus Prayer". It consists simply in uttering the single word "Jesus" (or "Lord Jesus", or "Lord Jesus Christ, have mercy on me, a sinner") in any situation, at any time and place, either aloud or silently".[12]

Prayer to God the Father:

"Pray then in this way Our Father in heaven, hallowed be your name." (Matthew 6:9 NRSV).

Discussion Questions:

1. To whom do you most often pray?
2. Do you ever pray to the Holy Spirit?

Memory Verse of The Week:

"You did not choose me but I chose you. And I appointed you to go and bear fruit, fruit that will last, so that the Father will give you whatever you ask him in my name." (John 15:16 NRSV).

For Whom Should We Pray - TLC Lesson 8

We should pray for ourselves:

A prayer for self is not a selfish prayer. We may pray for something for ourselves in order that God may be glorified by our receiving it. Jesus spent much time in prayer for Himself   (John 17:1-5)

We should pray for one another:

TLC Groups for Busy Disciples

Therefore confess your sins to one another, and pray for one another, so that you may be healed. The prayer of the righteous is powerful and effective." (James 5:16 NRSV).

We should pray for Pastors:

May the God of peace himself sanctify you entirely; and may your spirit and soul and body be kept sound and blameless at the coming of our Lord Jesus Christ. The one who calls you is faithful, and he will do this. Beloved, pray for us. (The Apostle Paul, 1 Thessalonians 5:23-25 NRSV).

We should pray for new Christians:

I ask not only on behalf of these, but also on behalf of those who will believe in me through their word, that they may all be one. As you, Father, are in me and I am in you, may they also be in us, so that the world may believe that you have sent me. (John 17:20-21 NRSV).

We should pray for the sick:

"Are any among you sick? They should call for the elders of the church and have them pray over them, anointing them with oil in the name of the Lord. The prayer of faith will save the sick, and the Lord will raise them up; and anyone who has committed sins will be forgiven." (James 5:14-15 NRSV)

We should pray for our children:

"People were bringing little children to him in order that he might touch them; and the disciples spoke sternly to them. But when Jesus saw this, he was indignant and said to them, "Let the little children come to me; do not stop them; for it is to such as these that the kingdom of God belongs. Truly I tell you, whoever does not

Chapter One Praying

receive the kingdom of God as a little child will never enter it." And he took them up in his arms, laid his hands on them, and   blessed them. "(Mark   10:13-16 NRSV).

We should pray for our leaders:

" First of all, then, I urge that supplications, prayers, intercessions, and thanksgivings be made for everyone, for kings and all who are in high positions, so that we may lead a quiet and peaceable life in all godliness and dignity." (1 Timothy 2:1-2 NRSV).

We should pray for our FRANgelism list.

Friends, Relatives, Associates, Neighbors.

Discussion Questions:

1. Who is on you Frangelism list?
2. When you pray for others, what do you say?

Memory Verse of the Week:

" First of all, then, I urge that supplications, prayers, intercessions, and thanksgivings be made for everyone." (1 Timothy 2:1 NRSV).

Five Kinds of Prayer - TLC Lesson 9

Many new member classes in local churches acquaint people with the various kinds of prayer by introducing them to the A.C.T.S. model of praying. ACTS is an **acronym** for adoration, confession, thanksgiving, and supplication. This is a very easy way to remember that prayer takes many forms and that growth in prayer involves personal application of those forms. I would suggest a fifth form of prayer called intercession, which in some ways overlaps with supplication but in other ways is distinct.

Adoration: The psalmist says, "You are awesome, God, in your sanctuaries. The God of Israel gives strength and power to his people. Praise is to God!**"** (Psalm 68:35 World English Bible **(WEB)**

TLC Groups for Busy Disciples

"Tell God, How awesome are your deeds!" (Psalm 66:3 World English Bible (WEB). Adoration is our way of telling God how much we appreciate God. It loves God for who God is. There are times when we need to stop asking God for things, or even thanking God for things and simply adore God. There are times when we tell our spouses, our children, our parents, our friends, "thank you for being you!", so it is with God!

Confession: (also known as penitence). "If we confess our sins, he is faithful and just, and will forgive our sins and cleanse us from all unrighteousness". (1 John 1:9 (RSV). "All have sinned and fall short of the glory of God" (Romans 3:23 RSV). Confession is telling God where we have fallen short. It is being very specific in telling God our sins and asking for God's forgiveness. It is asking God for help in turning away from future temptations. "No temptation has overtaken you that are not common to man. God is faithful, and he will **not** let you be tempted beyond your strength, but with the temptation will also provide the way of escape, that you may be able to endure it".(1 Corinthians 10:13. RSV).

Thanksgiving: "I will praise the name of God with a song; I will magnify him with thanksgiving *"glorify him with thanksgiving"* (Psalms 69:30 RSV). There are many reasons to thank God. Even in the midst of tragedy and hardship we are blessed. Thank God for God's forgiveness, guidance, wisdom, healing, providence, salvation, joy, strength, peace, and faithfulness. Thank God for freedom, family, food, friends, success, hope, plenty, the church, and a thousand other things.

Supplication: Supplication is defined as, "the action of asking or begging for something earnestly or humbly". "Have no anxiety about anything, but in everything by prayer and supplication with thanksgiving let your requests be made known to God". (Philippians 4:6 RSV). Supplication is asking God for the things we need in contrast to the things we want. It is earnestly seeking God's will in relation to all things, our life direction, our life work, our schooling, our health, and our interests

Intercession: Intercession is defined as, "the action of intervening on behalf of another. Intercession is similar to supplication except that it is praying for others rather than our selves. "I urge, then, first of all, that petitions, prayers, intercession and thanksgiving be made for all people". (1Timothy 2:1 RSV). "And pray in the Spirit on all

23

Chapter One Praying

occasions with all kinds of prayers and requests. With this in mind, be alert and always keep on praying for all the Lord's people". (Ephesians 6:18 RSV). We should pray for our pastors, church leaders, national and international leaders, FRAGelism list, families, children, and dozens of other people who come to mind.

Discussion Questions:

1). With which of the five kinds of prayer are you most familiar? Why?
2). With which of the five kinds of prayer are you least familiar? Why?

Memory Verse:

"No temptation has overtaken you that are not common to man. God is faithful, and he will **no**t let you be tempted beyond your strength, but with the temptation will also provide the way of escape, that you may be able to endure it".(1 Corinthians 10:13. RSV).

When You Don't Feel Like Praying - TLC Lesson 10

There are many times in life when we just don't' feel like praying. Perhaps we have suffered a major loss. Maybe we are simply exhausted. It is possible that something has made us angry with God. Sometimes people just go through a spiritual dry spell. We might be experiencing a period of apathy brought on by a bought of depression. Someone once said, "If you don't feel like praying, pray until you do!", perhaps easier said than done. So what shall we do when we simply don't feel like praying. Here are some suggestions.

Don't confuse prayer with performance. Prayer has little if anything to do with King James English, a super-spiritual-sounding voice or with one's eyes closed. Remember the elements of conversational prayer and just talk with God. Be real with God. Let your emotions out. Anger, confusion, pain, fear, doubt are all acceptable forms of prayer.

Tell God how you feel. Say, "God I really don't feel like talking to you right now". There are many times in life when we don't feel like talking to anybody, our spouse, our children, our friends. Some people draw back into a corner and hold their feelings in. This is not a healthy response. More often than not, your feelings will change if you talk about them. This is also true when talking with God.

Pray anyway, whether you feel like it or not. We don't send our children to school only on those days that they want to go. We don't go to our jobs only when we feel like it. So why should we offer our God any less honor and obedience than we offer our boss at work

Choose to listen. Sometimes you may be too tired or angry to hear much right away. Consciously choose to keep coming back into God's presence, perhaps after some rest. Simply be quiet. Sit in a quiet place and relax.

Read other prayers. Start with the Psalms. The Psalms are prayers. Take in their beauty. Read a book of prayers. Suggestion, "Prayers" by Michael Quoist.

Confess your Sins. "If we confess our sins, he who is faithful and just will forgive us our sins and cleanse us from all unrighteousness". (1 John 1:9 RSV).

Read The Bible or a Good Devotional Book. Prime your spiritual pump by focusing on the Word or on positive thoughts.

Take a Walk. Sometimes it helps to get out into nature, breath fresh air, listen quietly and be thankful for creation.
Discussion Questions:

Chapter One Praying

1). Describe a time in your life when you didn't feel like praying.

2). what has helped you when you didn't feel like praying?

Memory Verse:

"Likewise the Spirit helps us in our weakness; for we do not know how to pray as we ought, but that very Spirit intercedes with sighs too deep for words." (Romans 8:26 NRSV).

Where Faith Fits In - TLC Lesson 11

We now come to the final lesson in our TLC series on prayer. It is now time to ask the key question about prayer, "Where does faith fit in? I invite you, first of all, to hear what the Bible says.

What The Bible Says:

"Now faith is the assurance of things hoped for, the conviction of things not seen". (Hebrews 11:1 RSV).

"Therefore I tell you, whatever you ask in prayer, believe that you have received it, and it will be yours. (Mark 11:24 RSV)).

"For truly, I say to you, if you have faith as a grain of mustard seed, you will say to this mountain, 'Move from here to there,' and it will move; and nothing will be impossible to you." (Matthew 17:20 RSV).

"And Jesus answered them, "Truly, I say to you, if you have faith and never doubt, you will not only do what has been done to the fig tree, but even if you say to this mountain, 'Be taken up and cast into the sea,' it will be done". (Matthew 21:21   RSV)).

"For we walk by faith, not by sight". (2 Corinthians 5:7 RSV)

"For whatever is born of God overcomes the world; and this is the victory that overcomes the world, our faith". (1 John 5:4 RSV).

A Smorgasbord of Faith: Please listen quietly as the following quotes are read aloud. We will then move to our discussion questions.[59]

TLC Groups for Busy Disciples

Andrew Murray – "Faith expects from God what is beyond all expectation."

Dwight L. Moody – "A little faith will bring your soul to heaven, but a lot of faith will bring heaven to your soul."

Joni Erickson Tada – "Faith isn't the ability to believe long and far into the misty future. It's simply taking God at His Word   and taking the next step."

Matthew Barnett – "Faith believes that God is going to take you places before you even get there."

Rex Rouis – "Faith is hearing Jesus say, "Come." Believing is actually throwing your leg over the side of the boat."

Ralph Hodgson – "Some things have to be believed to be seen."

Unknown – "Faith isn't faith until it's all you're holding on to"

St. Thomas Aquinas – "To one who has faith, no explanation is necessary. To one without faith, no explanation is possible."

Martin Luther King, Jr – "Faith is taking the first step even when you don't see the whole staircase."

Charles Wesley – "Faith, mighty faith, the promise sees, and looks to God alone; Laughs at impossibilities, and cries it shall   be done."

Philip Yancey – "I have learned that faith means trusting in advance what will only make sense in reverse."

C.S. Lewis – "Faith is the art of holding on to things your reason has once accepted in spite of your changing moods"

Oswald Chambers – "Faith is deliberate confidence in the character of God whose ways you may not understand at the time."

Dietrich Bonhoeffer – "only the believer is obedient and only the obedient believe."

Saint Augustine – "Faith is to believe what you do not see; the reward of this faith is to see what you believe."

Unknown – "If God brings you to it, He will bring you through it."

Unknown – "Faith is the vision of the heart; it sees God in the dark as well as in the day."

Discussion Questions:

Chapter One Praying

1). having heard the above scriptures and quotes, where does faith fit in for you?

2). having heard the above scriptures and quotes, what doubts do you still have?

Memory Verse:

"Now faith is the assurance of things hoped for, the conviction of things not seen". – Hebrews 11:1. RSV

TLC Groups for Busy Disciples

~ Chapter Two - Witnessing ~

Chapter Two Witnessing

The Ultimate Walk across the Room - TLC Lesson 12

Forty three TLC lessons cover one year of study (with nine weeks off for holidays). The lessons are somewhat equally divided between the five membership vows of the United Methodist Church which ask each member to "be loyal to the United Methodist Church and support it with their Prayers, Presence, Gifts, Service and Witness".[13]

So what do we mean when we say, I will be loyal to the church with my witness? The definition of witness (as a noun) is "a person who testifies to a truth about an event that took place". The definition of witness (as a verb) is "to testify about the truth and reality of an event". A Christian witness is a person who believes in the death, resurrection, and Lordship of Jesus Christ and tells others about these events and truths. But how shall we go about witnessing?

If someone stopped you on the street and told you they were a Boston Red Sox fan and urged you to become one too, would that not strike you as just a wee bit odd? Would their enthusiasm and sincerity in telling about the team being last year's World Series winner impress you? And is it likely that their wearing a tee shirt with the team logo on it would make you want to embrace that particular baseball club as your own? Most of us would quickly become annoyed by such behavior and if it took place in the middle of New York City there would probably be some animosity aimed at the misguided zealot! So is this how we are supposed to witness for Christ--going forth with unbridled exuberance and telling everyone in sight about the Lord? Are we to be billboards with our clothes and cars covered with cutesy sayings, pictures and slogans advertising His worth? Must churches compete with each other to see who can have the cleverest comments on the signs out front? Please excuse me for being blunt, but that kind of "witnessing" often does more harm than good![14]

The average person takes about ten thousand steps a day. In a lifetime, that's four trips around the earth. However, the question of the hour is: Will he use his steps wisely? What if ten steps across a room could impact eternity? That thought stunned me as I listened to a Muslim tell his story of how he came to Christ. He was at a party, standing alone, when a Christ follower from the other side of the room broke away from his clique of friends and introduced himself. The two became instant friends. Over the course of time and after many spiritual conversations, the Muslim felt compelled to pray to God, and He gave His life to Jesus Christ. This happened all because a follower of Christ was willing to walk ten steps

TLC Groups for Busy Disciples

across a room.[15] so how do we actually go about witnessing (verb)? I have three suggestions.

1). <u>Live It</u>! It has been said that, "witnessing is not telling someone what you believe, but living your life in such a way that someone will ask you what you believe". The question then becomes, are you willing to tell them? Are you willing to walk across the room? Studies show that even very active Christians are often too busy or too timid to intentionally share their faith. Authors, like Bill Hybels[16], encourage Christians to intentionally take strategic steps to share their faith. (I.e. develop friendships, discover life stories, spend time with, pray for, and at the appropriate time <u>take the risk</u> of sharing the good news).

2). <u>Pray It</u>! TLC members consciously use FRANgelism lists to pray for others. Witnessing can begin by secretly putting someone on your FRANgelism list without telling them. Some have prayed for individuals for years without saying a word to them. But when the right moment comes, God will open up a conversation through the Holy Spirit. For this reason the Bible says, "Always be prepared to give an answer to anyone who asks you a reason for the hope that is in you, yet do it with gentleness and reverence". (1 Peter 3:15 Combination of KJV & RSV).

3). <u>Share It</u>! Ultimately all disciples are called to share the good news. Jesus gave his disciples a final encouraging word that we have come to know as the **<u>Great Commission</u>**. **"**And Jesus came and said to them, 'All authority in heaven and on earth has been given to me. Go therefore and make disciples of all nations, baptizing them in the name of the Father and of the Son and of the Holy Spirit, teaching them to observe all that I have commanded you; and lo, I am with you always, to the close of the age.'" (Matthew 28:18-20 RSV).

<u>Discussion Questions</u>:

1). How have you shared your faith over the years of your discipleship?
2). what most hinders you from witnessing?

<u>Memory Verse</u>:

"Always be prepared to give an answer to anyone who asks you a reason for the hope that is in you, yet do it with gentleness and reverence". (1 Peter 3:15 Combination of KJV & RSV)

Chapter Two Witnessing

The Meaning of Accepting Christ - TLC Lesson 13

We all have heard the phrase, "accepting Christ", but what does it mean to accept Christ? This idea has been related to several religious and/or theological catchphrases, for example, "to be born again," "to be saved', "to be regenerated". I believe that we can take several personal approaches to answering this question. One approach is what I would call:

The Contemporary Cultural approach. In modern culture some people actually think that the concept of "being born again" is some kind of ultra conservative religious concept embraced by fundamentalists and adopted by some popular political and celebrity personalities like President Jimmy Carter, Watergate conspirator Charles Colson, Bob Dylan, Little Richard, Johnny Cash, J C Penney, Randy Travis, C S Lewis, Charlie Daniels, and Mr. T., etc. Those who take this approach somehow have concluded that "being born again" means joining minds in some kind of cult like religious experience that is more a political and social statement than a valid religious outlook. People who take this view might be heard to say, "I'm not one of those born-againers", as though being born again means joining some political party or cult. Another approach is what I would call,

The Privatized "Christian?" Approach. People who take this approach tend to say. "Everyone has a right to believe as they choose, and we should not tell others what to believe, or be expected, by others, to say out loud what we believe." "After all we live in a democracy where everyone has a right to believe as they wish". "It is perfectly all right to interpret the meaning of accepting Christ for myself without help from anyone else." "I am not one of those bornagainers!" Another approach is what I would call,

The Seekers Approach. People who take this approach ask, "What does the Bible teach and what has the church historically believed?" People who take this approach are interested in doing online and/or Wikipedia searches using the phrases, "accepting Christ", "born again", "regeneration", "being saved", etc. As I have pursued this approach, the following has come to my attention, as to what accepting Christ means. Technically speaking the phrase "accepting Christ" does not appear in scripture. The idea of accepting Christ, Biblically speaking, is related to a series of experiential theological concepts expressed in key words like,

TLC Groups for Busy Disciples

PREVENIENT GRACE, JUSTIFICATION, REGENERATION (Born Again), FILLED_(with The Holy Spirit), SANCTIFICATION. All of these terms are in common usage within all Christian denominations Protestant and Catholic and are clearly explained in dictionaries and internet articles, keeping in mind that each group may have its varying slant. So let's consider these ideas one at a time.

1). Prevenient Grace. Prevenient grace is a Christian theological concept rooted in Arminian theology, though it appeared earlier in Catholic theology. It is divine grace that precedes human decision. It exists prior to and without reference to anything humans may have done. As humans are corrupted by the effects of sin, prevenient grace allows persons to engage their God-given free will to choose the salvation offered by God in Jesus Christ or to reject that salvation offer. Prevenient grace is embraced primarily by Arminian Christians who are influenced by the theology of Jacob Arminius or John Wesley. The United Methodist Book of Discipline (2004) defines prevenient grace as "the divine love that surrounds all humanity and proceeds any and all of our conscious impulses. This grace prompts our first wish to please God, our first glimmer of understanding concerning God's will, and our 'first slight transient conviction' of having sinned against God. God's grace also awakens in us an earnest longing for deliverance from sin and death and moves us toward repentance and faith.[17]

2). Justification. Justification is God's act of removing the guilt and penalty of sin while at the same time declaring a sinner righteous through Christ's atoning sacrifice. Righteousness from God is viewed as being credited to the sinner's account through faith alone, without works. God declares an unrighteous individual to be righteous, an act made possible because Christ was legally "made sin" while on the cross.[18] "For our sake he made him to be sin who knew no sin, so that in him we might become the righteousness of God". (2 Cor. 5:21 RSV). "We know that a person is justified not by the works of the law but through faith in Jesus Christ. And we have come to believe in Christ Jesus, so that we might be justified by faith in Christ, and not by doing the works of the law, because no one will be justified by the works of the law." (Galatians 2:16 RSV).

3). Regeneration. The term, in the Bible, is only found in Matthew 19:28 and Titus 3:5 . This word literally means a "new birth." The

Chapter Two Witnessing

Greek word so rendered (palingenesia) is used by classical writers with reference to the changes produced by the return of spring. In Matthew 19:28 the word is equivalent to the "restitution of all things". In Titus 3:5 it denotes that change of heart elsewhere spoken of as a passing from death to life (1 John 3:14); becoming a new creature in Christ Jesus (2 Corinthians 5:17); being born again (John 3:5); a renewal of the mind (Romans 12:2); a resurrection from the dead (Ephesians 2:6); a being quickened (Ephesians 2:1 Ephesians 2:5). This change is ascribed to the Holy Spirit. It originates not with man but with God (John 1:12 John 1:13 ; 1 John 2:29 ; 1 John 5:1 1 John 5:4). As to the nature of the change, it consists in the implanting of a new principle or disposition in the soul; the impartation of spiritual life to those who are by nature "dead in trespasses and sins." The necessity of such a change is emphatically affirmed in Scripture (John 3:3 ; Romans 7:18 ; 8:7-9 ; 1 Corinthians 2:14 ; Ephesians 2:1 ; 4:21-24).[19]

4). Filled (With The Holy Spirit). To be filled with the Holy Spirit is to be filled with Christ. I am controlled by Christ because the word "filling" means to be controlled. And if I am controlled -- not as a robot but as one who is led and empowered by the Spirit -- the Lord Jesus will walk around in my body and live His resurrection life in and through me.[20] To be filled with the Holy Spirit is to demonstrate the fruit of the Holy Spirit in one's life, (Galations 5:22-23), and to serve with the Gifts of the Holy Spirit.(1 Cor. 12:4-26).

5). Sanctification. Sanctification is the act or process of being set apart or made holy. United Methodists believe that sanctifying grace draws one toward the gift of Christian perfection, which Wesley described as a heart "habitually filled with the love of God and neighbor" and as "having the mind of Christ and walking as he walked".[21]

Discussion Questions:

1. How would you describe the meaning of accepting Christ from your own faith history?
2. How would you explain "accepting Christ" to someone else?

TLC Groups for Busy Disciples

<u>**Memory Verse**</u>:

"For by grace you have been saved through faith, and this is not your own doing; it is the gift of God not the result of works, so that no one may boast." (Ephesians 2:8-9 RSV).

Your Personal Story - TLC Lesson 14

Suppose you and your unconvinced neighbor have forged a friendship over the last few months. The more you interact, the more open and honest the relationship becomes. You've tested the spiritual waters a few times, and she knows that you are "into" God. One day, she asks you why you're so fired up about God. "Sure, I pray when I am in a bind," she elaborates, and I go to church at Christmas time... But that's about all I need. Why is this stuff so important to you?" How would you answer her? Do you have a response in mind?"[22]

The Bible says, "Quietly trust yourself to Christ your Lord, and if anybody asks why you believe as you do, be ready to tell him, and do it in a gentle and respectful way". (1 Peter 3:15 TLB).

Someone has said, "Witnessing is not about telling somebody what you believe, but waiting until someone asks you what you believe and then telling them".

There is a power in storytelling that can transform our lives. Our own life stories can be tools for making us whole; they gather up the parts of us and put them together in a way that gives our lives greater meaning than they had before we told our story. Our stories illustrate our inherent connectedness with others. In the life story of each person is a reflection of another's life story. In some mysterious, amazing way our stories and our lives are all tied together.[23]

"That is the power of a good story. It can encourage you, it can make you laugh, it can bring you joy. It will make you think, it will tap into your hidden emotions, and it can make you cry. The power of a story can also bring about healing, give you peace, and change your life!"[24]

Bill Hybels says in his book, "Just Walk across the Room", "let me offer a few coaching points on how to tell your story when someone sincerely wants to know why you're committed living for God".[25]

Chapter Two Witnessing

1). <u>Long-windedness</u>. Keep your story brief and allow your listener the chance to ask a few follow-up questions. Leave them wanting more and trust God to open up a dialogue if you are meant to say anything further about your journey. Three minutes or less is best.

2). <u>Fuzziness.</u> The only thing worse than a long story is a long story that is incoherent. Keeps your story simple containing one clear plot line that appropriately conveys the heartbeat of your faith journey.

3). <u>Religionsese</u>. Words like "salvation," "born again," "accepting Jesus," and "personal Lord and Savior," mean very little to people who aren't Christ followers. It takes a lot of work to expunge insider jargon from your story, but it's worth it. High praise from an unbelieving listener sounds like this, "I understand every word you just said."

4). <u>Superiority</u>. If you want to permanently repulsive a person from the things of God, try a little superiority on for size. Works every time.

5). <u>Before and After</u>. "When you tell your story, the critical contrast to draw for someone is this: what difference has Christ really made in your life? In other words, what were you like before Christ, and now what are you like after you've asked Christ to intervene? I promise you this: you will be absolutely amazed by the power of your own story once you have been diligent to hone and shape it and refine it. When you communicate your personal faith story with sincerity, you will see supernatural sparks fly as God uses it for his glory and your listeners good. Ready for your turn? The rules are the same: pull out a sheet of paper and get it done in 100 words or less.

<u>Discussion Questions</u>:

1). Who was most influential in leading you to faith in Christ?
2). What change happened in your life after you professed faith in Christ?

TLC Groups for Busy Disciples

Memory Verse:

"Therefore, if anyone is in Christ, he is a new creation;[the old has passed away, behold, the new has come." (2 Corinthians 5:17 RSV).

You're FRANgelism List TLC Lesson 15

Friends	Relatives
John	Pete
Mary	Lucy
Associates	Neighbors
Ann	Dale
Matt	Judy

Frangelism vs. Evangelism. Ask the average Christian how they feel about evangelism and they will often say something like, "it scares me." "Sometimes called "the e-word," as if evangelism is an unspeakable curse word, personal evangelism is generally not a regular discipline among believers in mainline churches because of associations with pushy street preachers. There are many reasons we choose not talk about our faith. We don't want to participate in high-pressure tactics or in the kinds of emotional manipulation seen on television. We don't want our friends to think we're foolish or simple-minded. Nor do we want to be perceived as combative or disrespectful of others' deeply held religious beliefs."[1] Frangelism, on the other hand is a different matter.

1). Frangelism is a Prayer Ministry. It is based on our belief in "Prevenient Grace." The United Methodist Book of Discipline (2004) defines prevenient grace as "the divine love that surrounds all humanity and proceeds any and all of our conscious impulses. This grace prompts our first wish to please God, our first glimmer of understanding concerning God's will, and our 'first slight transient conviction' of having sinned against God. God's grace also awakens in us an earnest longing for deliverance from sin and death and moves us toward repentance and faith." In simple terms this means that God's Spirit is already speaking to every human being before their name is put on a frangelism list. A close look at the United Methodist Hymnal reveals hymns related to this process.

Chapter Two Witnessing

The Power of the Holy Spirit is sung about in hymn numbers 328 to 336. Prevenient Grace is sung about in hymns 337 through 359. Most of the work of evangelism is done by the Holy Spirit. We need only to tap into the process (through prayer) of what God is already doing.

2). **Frangelism is Focused on Four Groups of People. Friends, Relatives. Associates, and Neighbors.**

Friends may include almost any one, class mates, people on your Christmas list, people listed in your church directory, a club membership, a group of boy scout or girl scout parents and leaders, a soccer team, a baseball team, a service club, etc.

Relatives might be a spouse, a child, an uncle or aunt, cousins, grandchildren, etc.

Associates are typically work mates, business associates, customers, business competitors, etc.

Neighbors are those who live in your neighborhood, across the street, next door, etc.

3). **Frangelism is Time Sensitive**. People may remain on your frangelism list for years without you ever speaking a word to them, or the Holy Spirit might set the stage for you to share your faith story in the next instant. So be ready! "Quietly trust yourself to Christ your Lord, and if anybody asks why you believe as you do, be ready to tell him, and do it in a gentle and respectful way". (1 Peter 3:15 TLB).

4). **Frangelism is Invitational.** When the moment is right for you to speak up you will know it. The Holy Spirit will set the stage. Be careful what you pray for, you might just get it – actually you will get it. Most modern day Christians are stuck on the witness model that says, "All I have to do is live the Christian life, I don't need to talk about my religion that is the pastor's job!" Not true, and deep in our hearts we all know it. So my friends, this is where the rubber meets the road concerning the future of the church of Jesus Christ in our modern world. All of us must speak up at the right moment!

5). **Frangelism is a Team Effort**. The key Scripture for all the work of the church is this, "and his gifts were that some should be apostles, some prophets, some evangelists, some pastors and teachers, to equip the saints for the work of ministry, for building up the body of Christ. (Ephesians 4:11 to 12 RSV). Let me spell it out,

TLC Groups for Busy Disciples

"if you are going to do FRANgelism (evangelism) effectively it is your pastors' calling to equip you to do this. This is God's plan! Pastors design a small group ministry plan. Group members invite other people to come to their small group. You pray and invite, pastor's design and plan. A repetitive process is put in place through which the church will grow and grow and grow. This worked for the New Testament church, for the early Methodist movement, and will work today. As a result, pastors and laity will commit themselves to do four things the rest of their lives until Jesus comes, worship weekly, attend Sunday school class weekly, attend a TLC group weekly and participate in a mission. This involves two hours and 59 minutes a week. Not bad considering what the grace of God is done for us.

Discussion Questions:

1. How is it going with your Frangelism list?
2. How can your Pastor(s) help you to be effective at Frangelism?

Memory Verse:

"Quietly trust yourself to Christ your Lord, and if anybody asks why you believe as you do, be ready to tell him, and do it in a   gentle and respectful way". (1 Peter 3:15 TLB).

How to Pray With Someone –TLC Lesson 16

One of the most satisfying experiences in my spiritual life has been the times when I was able to pray with someone. You might think that this experience is unique to pastors and professional church staff, but not so. Not long ago my wife and I had dinner with some old friends and the husband of the family, just before the meal, simply said," let me give thanks." He bowed his head and shared a simple prayer and then we ate. This experience is far more common than one might think. Even in public restaurants I routinely hear many Christians pray before meals. It is common place for me to pray with people in the hospital. Believe it or not, people actually expect me to pray with them when I visit them in the hospital. I wouldn't think of making a hospital visit without praying. And an even more important time to pray with someone is when the Holy Spirit has prepared their heart and your relationship to the point

Chapter Two Witnessing

where someone on your frangelism list opens up and says," will you pray with me?" What will you do when this happens?

Praying out loud with another person is often a challenge for Christians. This need not be so. All of us can learn to pray with others. Here are some basic principles to follow.

1). <u>Remember the methods of conversational prayer.</u>

    A). Everyday language.
    b). Short sentences.
    c). Sincere belief that God is listening.
    d). Brief and to the point.

2). <u>No need to be perfect or sound professional.</u> "The actual words of a prayer are for our benefit, not God's. I like to believe that God senses the intent behind our words regardless of the language in which the prayer is spoken. Hopefully, "It's the thought that counts" and some unseen energy takes the expectations of our thoughts and prayers, processes them and makes them useful to the people we've sent them to."[27]

3). <u>Listen carefully</u> to what the person says and focus your prayer on their need.

4). <u>Always ask</u> if you can pray with the person.

5). <u>Make the Prayer Sincere.</u> It matters little what the exact words are if you are sincere...

6). <u>Count on God.</u> Let you prayer reflect your belief that God is listening and know that God is working directly with the person with whom you are praying.

7). <u>Ask the person to pray silently</u> in their heart as you pray out loud.

8). <u>A sample prayer</u> goes like this; "I'd like to invite you to bow with me in prayer. If your' here and you have never put your trust in Christ. Simply to say, under your' breath, Jesus I trust in you. I

TLC Groups for Busy Disciples

believe in you. I believe that you love me. I wish to follow you and to live as your disciple."[28]

Discussion Questions:

1. What do you think it would be like to pray with someone?
2. What might hinder you from praying with someone?

Memory Verse:

"For God is my witness, whom I serve with my spirit in the gospel of his Son, that without ceasing I mention you always in my prayers." (Romans 1:9 RSV).

~ Chapter Three - Worshipping ~

TLC Groups for Busy Disciples

What is Worship? - TLC Lesson 17

The word "worship" is derived from the Old English word "woerthship", which literally means worth-ship, to give something its worth. So, when we worship God, we are proclaiming or giving God back God's worth. Christian worship is primarily about recognizing the worth of God, or honoring and praising God. In doing this we also remind ourselves who we are – the creation of a gracious, loving and all powerful being. One definition of worship is, "all that we are, responding to all that God is."

Worship is an active response to the character, words and actions of God, initiated by God's revelation and enabled by God's redemption, whereby the mind is transformed, and the heart is renewed, and actions are surrendered in accordance with God's will in order to declare God's infinite worthiness. In both Hebrew and Greek, there are two categories of words for worship. The first is about body language that demonstrates respect and submission; to bow down, to kneel, and to prostrate oneself. The second is about doing something for God that demonstrates sacrifice and obedience; to offer, to serve.[29]

The meaning of the New Testament Greek word most often translated "worship" is "to fall down before" or "bow down before." Worship is a state or an attitude of spirit. Since it's an internal, individual action, all the time in our lives, regardless of place or situation, is involved in worship. Christians worship all the time, seven days a week. When the Samaritan woman asked Jesus the proper place to worship he said, "The hour is coming, and now is, when the true worshipers will worship the Father in spirit and truth, for such the Father seeks to worship him. God is spirit, and those who worship him must worship in spirit and truth." (John 4:23 RSV)

1). We become like what we worship. Worship money, become a greedy person. Worship sex, become a lustful person. Worship power, become a corrupt person. Worship Jesus, become a Christ like person. The verb worship in Hebrew means to surrender, to fall down in submission, the way we would humble ourselves before a mighty king (see Psalms 95:6). Paul says that worship is the

Chapter Thee Worshipping

offering of our bodies as a sacrifice (See Romans 12:1).[30] we become like what we worship.

2). Cell and Celebration. While worship begins in the individual heart, true and complete worship is far more than just an individual act. Worship takes place in small groups (cells) when people gather to pray, study and grow in their relationship with God. Worship also takes place when the total congregation gathers for celebration. One of the signs of a maturing Christian is when one says," I will show up at church not just for myself but for others." Researchers have discovered that people like to worship in large congregations because they cannot sing. They love the uplifting power of congregational singing, but like to have their own voices overpowered by many voices. An old poem about life's difficulties gives this advice, when things get really tough, "then nestle your hand in your father's, and sing, if you can, as you go; your song may cheer someone behind you, whose courage is sinking low, and well, if your lips do quiver God will love you better so." You never know who will be uplifted by your presence in church (singing) next Sunday!

3). Objective and Subjective Worship. Objective hymns are focused on God, Jesus or the Holy Spirit. Hymns like "How Great Thou Art", "When Morning Gilds the Skies" (May Jesus Christ be praised), "Spirit of The Living God", draw our attention to the person of God, to praising God, to serving God, to honoring God, and to God's greatness and goodness. Subjective hymns focus on our personal experience of God and are our testimony to salvation. Hymns like "Amazing Grace", "Victory in Jesus", "Sweet Hour of Prayer", "And Can it Be That I Should Gain", and "What a Friend we Have in Jesus", are more subjective hymns that speak of our personal relationship with God. Pastors will often try to seek a balance between objective and subjective worship when planning a worship service.

4). **The Purpose of Worship.** The word "church" comes from the Greek word *ekklesia* which is defined as "an assembly" or "called-out ones." The root meaning of "church" is not that of a building, but of people. According to the Bible, the church is the body of Christ— all those who have placed their faith in Jesus Christ for salvation. The local church is where the members of the universal church can

TLC Groups for Busy Disciples

fully apply the "body" principles of 1 Corinthians chapter 12: encouraging, teaching, and building one another up in the knowledge and grace of the Lord Jesus Christ. Worship is the Assembly of God's people for preparation for service to the world.

Discussion Questions:

1. Why do you attend church?
2. Why do you think God wants you to attend church?

Memory Verse:

"God is spirit, and those who worship him must worship in spirit and truth." (John 4:24 RSV)

Who Do We Worship? - TLC Lesson 18

On the suggestion of one pastor, I looked up the word god (small g) on the Internet. I found this interesting site called, "God Checker". The site is described as" The Legendary Encyclopedia, Your Guide to The Gods". It says you can "discover almost 4000 god's, goddesses, and spirits from around the world". It even asks, "Who's the most popular?" Then it says, "See the top 10 gods here."

It sounds strange to use the word "idolatry" in our modern culture. We Christians tend to think that idolatry was a phenomenon in Old Testament times related to things like the golden calf and Baal worship. But idolatry is alive and well in the 21st century. The definition of idolatry, according to Webster, is "the worship of idols or excessive devotion to, or reverence for some person or thing." An idol is anything that replaces the one, true God. Our modern idols are many and varied. Idolatry is a matter of the heart—pride, self-centeredness, greed, gluttony, a love for possessions and ultimately rebellion against God. The Bible teaches that an idol is anything that is more important than God. Anything, whether physical or not, that is more important to a Christian than God is an idol.

Jesus had a discussion with the Samaritan woman at the well. She had questions about true worship. "Our fathers worshiped on this

Chapter Thee Worshipping

mountain; and you say that in Jerusalem is the place where men ought to worship." Jesus said to her, "Woman, believe me, the hour is coming when neither on this mountain nor in Jerusalem will you worship the Father. You worship what you do not know; we worship what we know, for salvation is from the Jews. But the hour is coming, and now is, when the true worshipers will worship the Father in spirit and truth, for such the Father seeks to worship him. God is spirit, and those who worship him must worship in spirit and truth." (John 4:20-24 RSV).

The discussion of "who do we worship" is similar to the TLC Lesson 7 topic of "to whom should we pray?" "All prayer should be directed to our triune God—Father, Son, and Holy Spirit. The Bible teaches that we can pray to one or all three, because all three are one". The same is true of worship.

A quick glance at the United Methodist hymnal reveals that hymns 57 through 152 are listed under the general category of "the glory of the triune God". Take for example hymn number 61, "Come, Thou Almighty King".

Come, Thou almighty King, Help us Thy Name to sing, help us to praise! Father all glorious, o'er all victorious, Come and reign over us, Ancient of Days!

Jesus, our Lord, arise, Scatter our enemies, and make them fall; Let Thine almighty aid our sure defense be made, Souls on Thee be stayed; Lord, hear our call.

Come, holy Comforter, Thy sacred witness bear in this glad hour; Thou Who almighty art, now rule in every heart, And ne'er from us depart, Spirit of power.

To Thee, great One in Three, Eternal praises be, hence, evermore; Thy sovereign majesty may we in glory see, And to eternity love and adore![31]

Discussion Questions:

TLC Groups for Busy Disciples

1. What are some of the idols that get in the way of true worship in our lives today?
2. What do we need to keep us focused on true worship?

<u>Memory Verse</u>:

"God is spirit, and those who worship him must worship in spirit and truth." (John 4:24 RSV).

Worship, More Than a Habit. - TLC lesson 19

David Santistevan in an online article asks, "How can we keep ourselves from simply running to Jesus when there's a tragedy and make (worship) more second nature every single day? He suggests that we consider our five senses by asking ourselves:
Are you using your eyes to constantly see more of His glory and stand more in awe?
Are you using your ears to be tuned into the voice of the Holy Spirit?
Are you using your mind to comprehend the mysteries of God through the Bible?
Are you tasting and seeing that God is good?
Are you feeling strong affections for Christ deep in your bones?
Are you reaching out and extending God's grace to the world?[32]

Worship leader, Matt Redman wrote a revolutionary worship song entitled "The Heart of Worship" based on a felt need for the church to return to the spirit of true worship. Reflect for a moment on these challenging words, "When the music fades, all is stripped away, and I simply come, Longing just to bring, Something that's of worth, That will bless Your heart, I'll bring You more than a song, For a song in itself, Is not what You have required, You search much deeper within, Through the way things appear, You're looking into my heart, I'm coming back to the heart of worship, And it's all about You, It's all about You, Jesus, I'm sorry, Lord, for the thing I've made it, When it's all about You,, It's all about You,Jesus".[33]

Our modern church culture has developed some strange and challenging worship habits. In talking with modern-day church

Chapter Thee Worshipping

members, as a pastor, I hear some very candid comments about worship attendance.

1). One church member confided in me, "I really only attend worship on Christmas and Easter". I think he really believed he was scoring points with me by being honest. Little did he know that in my mind I was thinking," How does that fit with the membership vow you took saying that "I will be loyal to the church with my presence (worship)?"

2). Another church member confided in me," I haven't been back to church since the pastor I liked moved". Again, points for honesty? Same question in my mind, "what about your vow?"

3). Another church member said, "I just have so many things to do that I can't make it to church very often". Again, points for honesty? The average church member attends worship one Sunday per month according to the latest national surveys. Same question from me, "what about your vow?"

4). Another church member shared with me, "my life has been so full of troubles lately that I thought I needed to get back to church". George W. Cornell says, "A turn to religion is natural in periods of turmoil. Religious impulses usually quicken in time of crisis, and facing uncontrollable events, people tend to reach for transcendent help. Church attendance rises and people pray more with the advent of war".[34] so, should a pastor pray for troubled times to come?

The author of Hebrews writes, "Not neglecting to meet together, as is the habit of some, but encouraging one another, and all the more as you see the Day drawing near". (Hebrews 10:25 RSV). Commentator Adam Clark suggests that this "likely means private religious meetings, for the purpose of mutual exhortation".[35] this verse is often quoted as an exhortation to attend worship regularly. Although worship services in the modern day sense had not yet been established, it is still a good Bible verse to encourage faithful worship attendance as a way of encouraging each other.

Discussion Questions:

TLC Groups for Busy Disciples

1. Why do you think regular worship attendance is important?
2. What is your opinion about church members neglecting to attend worship?

<u>**Memory Verse**</u>:

"Not neglecting to meet together, as is the habit of some, but encouraging one another, and all the more as you see the Day drawing near". (Hebrews 10:25 RSV).

Can/Should Worship Be Fun? - TLC Lesson 20

A woman began attending worship services regularly. She attended every week for several months and then suddenly disappeared before joining the church. The pastor did not see her for a while until one day he ran into her in a store. He mentioned that he had missed seeing her at church. She explained that she had joined another congregation. He used the opportunity to do a brief exit interview to learn why she was unsatisfied with the church. She responded with surprising honesty. "Pastor, I don't want to hurt your feelings, but it is mostly your fault." "I came to your church for a while and tried to give it a fair chance. But, to tell you the truth, I have problems with your approach to sermons and worship. You see, I realized that while attending your church I was experiencing a dangerous shift in my life. I started liking church—even looking forward to Sundays. Coming to your church, I was having fun. Since I knew that it was wrong to enjoy worship, I switched to a church where attending worship feels like I am fulfilling my duty for God."[36]

This brief story raises an interesting question about worship. Can or should worship be fun? Over the years I have asked a number of youth to describe Sunday morning worship in one word. Almost unanimously the answer is "boring!" We could ask a different question in this context, "does worship need to be boring?"

I looked up "fun" on my desktop thesaurus; the first meaning that came up was "enjoyable." If the question is, "Can worshipping God be enjoyable?" Then the answer is absolutely yes!

49

Chapter Thee Worshipping

Bob Kauflin says in an online article, "When my children were growing up, I wanted them to look forward to singing worship songs, and not see a relationship with God as something that was only serious, sober, and solemn. After all, singing to God is meant to be pleasant (Ps. 135:3; Ps. 147:1 RSV). David danced before the Lord with all his might as he brought the ark back to Jerusalem (2 Sam. 6:12-15 RSV). The Psalmist was glad when they said to him, "Let us go up to the house of the Lord" (Ps. 122:1 RSV). So yes, when defined as enjoyment and not seen as the only aspect of worship, worshipping God can be *very* "fun."[37]

The Psalmist said, "Our mouths were filled with laughter, our tongues with songs of joy. Then it was said among the nations, "The LORD has done great things for them." The LORD has done great things for us, and we are filled with joy." (Psalms 126:2-3 RSV)

God gave us so much in this world to take pleasure and find joy in, why do we pretend to ignore that in church as if we are ashamed of God's gifts? Let's have fun in church, or at least stop hiding and start embracing and celebrating the holiness of how God created us to experience and enjoy pleasure. We all already admit such things are from God, why do we act otherwise when we gather as the body of Christ? Fun is a strategic imperative for the church today. Gospel oriented churches need to be the sort of place where joy, goodness and fun abound. When people interact with us they should walk away with a smile on their face.[38]

Discussion Questions:

1. Do you think worship should be enjoyable (fun)? Why?
2. What makes worship enjoyable for you?
3. What makes worship boring for you?

Memory Verse:

Shout joyfully to the LORD, all the earth. Serve the LORD with gladness; Come before Him with joyful singing.(Psalms 100:1-2 RSV).

TLC Groups for Busy Disciples

Why Is Corporate Worship Important? - TLC Lesson 21

Some people joke about the "Bedside Baptists" who attend the "Chapel of the Tube" on Sunday mornings. But it's more than a joke. Many people refuse to get near a church unless their nephew is playing the role of a sheep in the Christmas pageant! They claim they can get more out of a walk in the woods than from the typical sermon. Can a Christian survive apart from a church? Some Christians have no choice. They are trapped in a hospital bed, or working in an isolated area where no church exists. And God is certainly sufficient to care for their needs. You can still get to heaven if you can't go to church. But even though it's technically possible to live the Christian life in isolation, it's certainly not the norm. When you become a Christian, you are called into a relationship with God (1 Corinthians 1:9). But I John 1:3 makes it clear that we enter a fellowship that goes two ways: with God and with other Christians. The New Testament never divides Christians into the church members and the non-church members. All the way through, it assumes that everybody participates in their local assembly. It gives no samples of Christians who belong to the "universal church" but have no link with a local church. One scholar has said that "any idea…of enjoying salvation or being a Christian in isolation is foreign to the New Testament writings" (Alan Stibbs, *God's Church*, p. 92).[39]

So why is attending Sunday morning worship so important? Here are some suggestions.

1). It Helps Others. The truth be told, we live in a self-centered society. We have been called, the "me generation". Almost anything we do, anything we join, anything we contribute to, and anything we take interest in is preceded by the implied question, "what's in it for me?" Many people have stopped going to church because they say, "I don't get anything out of it". It seems we have forgotten that the church began with a sacrifice, "God so loved the world that he gave his only begotten son" (John 3:16 RSV). We've got it backwards. We should go to church, not for what we get out of it, but for what our presence can do for others. Other Christians need your support. They want to hear you singing on Sunday morning. They need a hug and a handshake. They need to know that you stand with them in the face of life's trials, disappointments, victories, successes,

Chapter Thee Worshipping

illnesses, and mission projects. They want to hear you say, "You're not in this alone, I'm here to help!"

2). It Feeds Your Soul. The Apostle Paul wrote to the church in Rome, "For the kingdom of God is not food and drink but righteousness and peace and joy in the Holy Spirit. (Romans 14:17 RSV). May the God of hope fill you with all joy and peace in believing, so that by the power of the Holy Spirit you may abound in hope. (Romans 15:13 RSV). The experience of singing congregational hymns, praying with other Christians, hearing God's word read and preached, listening to a beautiful choir anthem, sharing in tithes offerings, fulfilling your personal mission is all a part of the wonderful experience we call corporate worship. All of this lifts the soul!

3). It Keeps You Accountable. It is so easy to become discouraged, lose direction, fall into temptation, give up on life, and become confused when we try to "go it alone" in life. Being committed to a loving fellowship of Christian believers is a sure way to keep us on track. "Therefore confess your sins to one another, and pray for one another, that you may be healed. My brethren, if any one among you wanders from the truth and someone brings him back, let him know that whoever brings back a sinner from the error of his way will save his soul from death and will cover a multitude of sins". (James 5:16,19-20 RSV).

4). It Fulfills Your Purpose. Not only are individual human beings created in the image of God, they are created for the purpose of God. St. Augustine said years ago, "Restless is the heart until it finds rest in thee". Every human life has a "God destiny". The Bible says, "And his gifts were that some should be apostles, some prophets, some evangelists, some pastors and teachers, to equip the saints for the work of ministry, for building up the body of Christ". (Ephesians 4:11-12 RSV). It is in the context or corporate worship and Christian fellowship that individual spiritual gifts, are discovered, enhanced, and deployed.

Discussion Questions:

1. How would you describe the importance of worship attendance in your life?
2. How do you feel about "inactive church members?"

TLC Groups for Busy Disciples

<u>**Memory Verse:**</u>

"I was glad when they said to me; Let us go to the house of the Lord!" (Psalm 122:1 RSV).

~ Chapter Four - Serving ~

TLC Groups for Busy Disciples

The Meaning of Spiritual Gifts -TLC Lesson 22

Spiritual gifts are endowments given by the Holy Spirit. These are supernatural graces which enable individual Christians to do ministry within the church and world. They are described in the New Testament primarily in 1 Corinthians 12, Romans 12, and Ephesians 4 and are briefly described in various other passages. There are two major opposing theological positions on their nature. One is that they ceased at the end of the Apostolic Age with the death of the Apostles. The other view is that the spiritual gifts have remained active throughout history and are still active today. The first view is called cessationism and the second view is called continuationism.

From these scriptural passages, Christians understand the spiritual gifts to be enablements or capacities that are divinely bestowed upon individuals. Because they are freely given by God, these cannot be earned or merited. Though worked through individuals, these are operations or manifestations of the Holy Spirit—not of the gifted person. They are to be used for the benefit of others, and in a sense they are granted to the church as a whole more than they are given to individuals. There is diversity in their distribution—an individual will not possess all of the gifts. The purpose of the spiritual gifts is to edify (build up), exhort (encourage), and comfort the church.[40]

Cessationism is held by some Protestants, especially from the Calvinist tradition, who believe that the gifts were limited to early Christianity and "ceased" afterward. Other Protestants adhere to the continuationist position, believing that the spiritual gifts are still active today. Roman Catholicism and Eastern Orthodoxy also continue to believe in and make use of the spiritual gifts.

Spiritual gifts are distinguished from other graces of the Holy Spirit, such as the fruit of the Spirit, in that spiritual gifts are given individually as God wills and the "fruit" (singular) of the Holy Spirit is given as a cluster of nine graces that are given to all Christians. The fruit of the Spirit is love, joy, peace, patience, kindness, goodness, faithfulness, gentleness, and self-control. (Galatians 5:22 RSV). Dr.

Chapter Four Serving

Kenneth Kinghorn says that a careful reading of the above mentioned scriptures yields five basic principles regarding spiritual gifts.

1). God imparts spiritual gifts according to his divine grace; they cannot be earned through human merit.

2). God gives spiritual gifts according to his own discretion; he is not bound by man's wishes.

3). God wills that every Christian exercise spiritual gifts; these divine enablings are not limited to a few believers.

4). God provides gifts for the purpose of ministry and service; they are not given in order to draw attention to man or to satisfy his ego.

5). God intends that ministry of the church be accomplished through spiritual gifts; human talents are not adequate for spiritual ministry.[41]

Discussion Questions:

1). What has been your experience with spiritual gifts?
2). What questions do you have regarding spiritual gifts?
3). How do you think spiritual gifts can help our church?

Memory Verse:

"There are different kinds of gifts, but the same Spirit distributes them. There are different kinds of service, but the same Lord". (1 Corinthians 12:5-6 RSV).

Discovering Your Spiritual Gifts - TLC Lesson 23

The primary Scriptures which describe spiritual gifts are found in 1 Corinthians 12, Romans 12, and Ephesians 4. "Now there are varieties of gifts, but the same Spirit; and there are varieties of service, but the same Lord; and there are varieties of working, but it is the same God who inspires them all in every one. To each is given the manifestation of the Spirit for the common good. To one is given through the Spirit the utterance of wisdom, and to another the utterance of knowledge according to the same Spirit, to another faith by the same Spirit, to another gifts of healing by the one Spirit, to another the working of miracles, to another prophecy, to another the ability to distinguish between spirits, to another various kinds of tongues, to another the interpretation of tongues. All these are inspired by one and the same Spirit, who apportions to each one individually as he wills". (1 Corinthians 12:4-11 RSV).

"So we, though many, are one body in Christ, and individually members one of another. Having gifts that differ according to the grace given to us, let us use them: if prophecy, in proportion to our faith; if service, in our serving; he who teaches, in his teaching; he who exhorts, in his exhortation; he who contributes, in liberality; he who gives aid, with zeal; he who does acts of mercy, with cheerfulness. (Romans 12:5-8 RSV).

"And his gifts were that some should be apostles, some prophets, some evangelists, some pastors and teachers, to equip the saints for the work of ministry, for building up the body of Christ, until we all attain to the unity of the faith and of the knowledge of the Son of God, to mature manhood, to the measure of the stature of the fullness of Christ; so that we may no longer be children, tossed to and fro and carried about with every wind of doctrine, by the cunning of men, by their craftiness in deceitful wiles. Rather, speaking the truth in love, we are to grow up in every way into him who is the head, into Christ, from whom the whole body, joined and knit together by every joint with which it is supplied, when each part is working properly, makes bodily growth and up-builds itself in love". (Ephesians 4: 11-16 RSV).

Here are some practical ways to discover your spiritual gifts.

1). Acknowledge that God has given you spiritual gifts.

2). Pray about it. Ask God to show you your God given gifts. Use the power of prayer and introspection to sense what you are called to be and do.

3). Study the Bible. Read over the scriptures related to spiritual gifts multiple times and seek to understand what the Bible actually says.

4). Take a spiritual gifts survey or inventory. This is not fool-proof or totally conclusive but it will give you something to think about. The

Chapter Four Serving

United Methodist Church has a spiritual gifts survey at the following web site, (http://www.umc.org/what-we-believe/spiritual-gifts-online-assessment).

5). Ask for input from Christians friends in a small group.

6). Volunteer at church to see how you fit.

7). Read a book or take a course on spiritual gifts. (i.e. "Gifts of the Spirit" by Kenneth Cain Kinghorn).
8). Talk with your pastor.

Discussion Questions:

1). What are some of your spiritual gifts?
2). What areas of ministry or service interest you in our local church?

Memory Verse:

"So we, though many, are one body in Christ, and individually members one of another. Having gifts that differ according to the grace given to us, let us use them" (Romans 12:5 RSV).

The Enabling Gifts - TLC Lesson 24

The enabling gifts are those used to strengthen the ministry of the church by building up the spiritual gifts of other members of the Body of Christ. These include:

Spiritual Gift # 2 Evangelism: Evangelism is the ability to be unusually effective in leading unbelievers to a saving knowledge of Christ. People with this gift are good at making new disciples. People with this gift are usually very outgoing, enthusiastic, good listeners, and comfortable talking about their personal faith. They frequently think about the unchurched and maintain a very detailed FRANgelism list. They have a solid knowledge of the Bible and are very good at learning memory verses. Every Christian is called to

TLC Groups for Busy Disciples

share their faith and to do evangelism, but the person with the gift of evangelism has an extraordinary ability to share faith and to win others to faith. The gift of evangelism is mentioned in (Ephesians 4:11 RSV).

Spiritual Gift # 3 Exhortation: Exhortation is the gift of motivating others to respond to Christian faith by providing timely words of counsel, encouragement, and consolation. This gift includes acts of standing by, sitting with, guiding, strengthening, inspiring, consoling, and comforting others. People with this gift stand ready to give an encouraging word, a needed hug, a listening ear, or a needed insight. Extorters have a deep intuition about the needs of others and are able to bring needed instruction, motivation, and direction at the exact moment it is needed. The gift of exhortation is mentioned in (Romans 12:8 RSV).

Spiritual Gift # 11 Prophecy: The gift of prophecy is the ability to receive and proclaim a message from God. It is the ability to proclaim God's truth in a way relevant to current situations and to envision how God would will things to change. This could involve foretelling future events, though its primary purpose is forthtelling. One who prophesies speaks to people for their strengthening, encouragement, and consolation. The prophet does not worry about what others think. The profit is usually not inhibited and is very expressive. The prophet does not feel the need to be popular. The prophet believes that God has a plan for every person. The prophet is not very patient with people's problems. Prophecy in the contemporary church has much more to do with giving guidance to the body of Christ or to individuals than it do to foretelling the future. Prophecy is often associated with powerful preaching. The gift is mentioned in (1 Corinthians 12:10, 29 and Ephesians 4:11 RSV).

Spiritual Gift # 13 Shepherd: This gift is the ability to guide and care for other Christians as they experience spiritual growth. This is also called pastor/shepherd and can relate to the call to become an ordained pastor. This gift also is seen in laypersons with shepherding skills. Not all shepherds are ordained. Many shepherds are dedicated laypersons. People with this gift are usually very patient. They are good listeners. They are a jack of all trades. They often pray for others. They love people. They are viewed as authoritative by others. They are more leaders than followers. They are expressive, composed, and sensitive. They like to study. They have a burden to see others learn and grow. See (Ephesians 4:11 RSV).

Spiritual Gift #14 Teacher: The spiritual gift of teaching is the ability to clearly explain and effectively apply the truth of God's word so that others will learn. This requires the capacity to accurately interpret Scripture, engage in necessary research, and organize the results in a way that is easily communicated. Teachers love to study the Bible. When they teach, others are motivated to learn more about the Bible and their faith. They like to relate God's truth to life in a way that helps people grow and develop. Teachers like to work with groups of people. They are usually technical and methodical. They like charts, graphs, and lists. They have an organized system to store facts. The gift of teaching is referred to in 1 Corinthians 12:28, and Ephesians 4:11. This gift is also linked to the gift of shepherd and is expressed in the book of Ephesians as pastor/teacher.

Discussion Questions:

1). How have you personally experienced one or more of the enabling gifts?
2). When have you experienced or seen the enabling gifts present in others in the church?

Memory Verse:

"And his gifts were that some should be apostles, some prophets, some evangelists, some pastors and teachers, to equip the saints for the work of ministry, for building up the body of Christ". (Ephesians 4:11-12 RSV).

The Serving Gifts - TLC Lesson 25

The serving gifts compliment the enabling gifts and act as supporting gifts that work alongside of those who enable the church. These include gifts that are person centered like healing, helps, and mercy and gifts that are congregation centered like leadership and service (deacons).

Spiritual Gift #6 Healing: Healing is the ability to call on God for the curing of illnesses, relationships, emotions, attitudes, and wounded souls. Inner healing, or healing of memories is also associated with this gift. People with this gift believe in the power of prayer and in miracles. They tend to have an intuitive sense about the needs of people. They feel a calling to pray with people. They believe in the combined power of prayer, modern medicine, and the medical community. They also know that sometimes people are not healed. They know that the lack of healing does not mean that the sick person has sinned, but that God has something different in mind. They also believe strongly that death is the ultimate healing and that the resurrection is the ultimate act of God making all things whole. The specific reference to the spiritual gift of healing is 1 Corinthians 12:9.

Spiritual Gift # 7 helps: This gift comes from the Greek word that means, "To aid and assist another in need". It is mentioned only once in the New Testament and appears to be distinct from the gift of service. Some suggest that while the gift of service is more group oriented, the gift of helps is more people oriented. The gift is reciprocal in that the receiver does as much for the giver as the giver does to the receiver. Helpers center on the needs of another person or persons but service centers on the worship of God. People with this gift give from their skills, talents, and energy to help others who have an apparent need. They enjoy one-on-one ministry over large groups. These people tend to notice and assist with practical tasks that need to be done. It is mentioned once only in 1 Corinthians 12:28.

Spiritual Gift #9 Leadership: This gift is the ability to motivate, coordinate, and direct the efforts of others in doing God's work. People with this gift are able to get people to work together toward a goal. They have a vision for the future. They are able to give directions to others in a caring way that creates willing followers. They are not afraid to take risks. They are able to make unpopular decisions. They work well with conflict. They see leadership as different from management. Management, like administration, is the

Chapter Four Serving

ability to organize information or material to work efficiently for the body of Christ. Leadership is the ability to coordinate the efforts of the body of Christ to achieve the goals outlined in the information. Leaders are more interested in effectiveness than efficiency. Good leaders look for a balance between management and vision. The biblical reference for leadership is Romans 12:8

Spiritual Gift # 10 Mercy: The gift of mercy is the ability to deeply empathize with others and to engage in compassionate acts on behalf of people who are suffering physical, mental, or emotional distress. Those with this gift manifest concern and show kindness toward people who are often overlooked. All Christians are called to have mercy, but some have an extraordinary gift that causes them to feel the discomfort of others. Mercy showers are quick to come to the aid of people in need. The gift of mercy is mentioned in 2 Corinthians 5:19.

Spiritual Gift # 12 Service: The gift of service comes from the Greek word meaning "deacon" and relates to special acts of servanthood. This gift, unlike the gift of helps, is worship centered whereas the gift of helps is person centered. People with this gift have a strong sense of loyalty to their local church. They enjoy manual tasks and are usually easy-going. They are good listeners and strong team players. They would rather be on a committee then serve as the leader. They feel called to lay ministry. They will stick to tasks until they are completed. They view their life work as a form of worship and live for the building up of their church. See Romans 12:7.

Discussion Questions:

1). How have you personally experienced one or more of the serving gifts?
2). When have you experienced or seen the serving gifts present in others in the church

Memory Verse:

"Having gifts that differ according to the grace given to us, let us use them: if service, in our serving". (Romans 12:6-7 RSV

TLC Groups for Busy Disciples

The Other Gifts - TLC Lesson 26

There are many spiritual gifts listed or implied in the Bible. Some spiritual gift surveys include as many as 27 gifts of the Spirit. Some theologians suggest that there could be even more spiritual gifts than are listed in the Bible. I have taken the approach of listing the 15 most commonly recognized and used gifts in the churches. I believe that it is important to distinguish between a talent and a gift.

A talent is a natural ability and a gift is a supernatural ability. People are born with a talent, but only the Holy Spirit can give people spiritual gifts. Both talents and gifts can be developed with practice. For example, playing the piano is a talent, using this talent to reach others for Christ is the gift of evangelism.

Spiritual Gift # 1 Administration: Administration is the ability to organize information, events, or material to work efficiently for the body of Christ. The administrator can see a local church's ministries in full scope, past present and future. He or she likes to work with a plan. Administrators usually are well-organized, disciplined, and like everything in its place. They tend to be task oriented and hard-working. He or she likes to do detailed work and seldom procrastinates. Administrators are good with charts, lists, and reports. Administrators are like managers and focus predominantly on organization, details, schedules and skills instead of on the relationships and people involved. The role of administrator is sometimes confused with the role of leader. Leaders work with relationships, vision, risk-taking and overall planning. Leaders work to put a plan in place. Administrators work to keep the plan working well. The word for administrator appears only one time in the New Testament in (1 Corinthians 12:28). Leaders help the church to do the right things while administrators work with making things efficient.

Spiritual Gift # 4 Faith: This is the ability to have a vision for what God wants to be done and to confidently believe that it will be accomplished in spite of circumstances and appearances to the contrary. The gift of faith transforms vision into reality. Every Christian has faith but the gift of faith is an extraordinary ability to believe and encourage belief in others in the face of challenging

63

and difficult circumstances. People with the faith gift are able to support others who have doubts. They believe deeply in the power of prayer and are not discouraged easily. They believe in miracles and are incurable optimists. They are willing to take risks in supporting the church because they believe God will see them through. This gift is mentioned in (1 Corinthians 12:9).

Spiritual Gift # 5 Giving: The gift of giving is the ability to contribute material resources with generosity and cheerfulness for the benefit of others to the glory of God. Christians with this gift need not be wealthy. This gift, is sometimes translated "generosity" and means "to turn over", to give over", or "to share". All Christians are called to give but God gives certain people an extraordinary sense of others' needs and the power to do something about it. People with this gift tend to have very cheerful hearts and have an overwhelming desire to give abundantly. People with this gift like to give quietly and without acknowledgment. The gift of giving is mentioned in (Romans 12:8).

Spiritual Gift # 8 Knowledge: This gift is the ability to discover, analyze, and systematize truth for the benefit of others and for the advancement of God's kingdom. People with this gift enjoy studying the Bible and other books to gain information about spiritual things. They are very analytical. They are able to understand complicated things. They know how to give simple clear directions and they are very logical persons. Others often ask them to explain things. They are often able to articulate complex ideas in simple words and phrases. The gift of knowledge is mentioned in (1 Corinthians 12:8).

Spiritual Gift # 15 Wisdom: The gift of wisdom is the ability to apply the principles of the Word of God in a practical way to specific situations and to recommend the best course of action at the best time. The exercise of this gift skillfully distills insight and discernment into excellent advice. People with this gift show a wide range of intelligence about many subjects and ministries. These people are able to act, speak, write, or apply God's eternal truths to the concrete realities of daily living in ministering to others. People with this gift are not afraid of complex or paradoxical situations. They are often asked for advice. This gift is mentioned in (1 Corinthians 12:8).

TLC Groups for Busy Disciples

Discussion Questions:

1). How have you personally experienced one or more of these gifts?
2). When have you experienced or seen these gifts present in others in the church?

Memory Verse:

"Rejoice in your hope, be patient in tribulation, be constant in prayer. Contribute to the needs of the saints, practice hospitality". (Romans 12:12-13 RSV).

Spiritual Gifts and the Church -TLC Lesson 27

What follows is straight from the heart of a pastor with fifty three years of ministry experience. My goal is to share what I have learned about spiritual gifts from reading the Bible, Christian books, and discussing the topic with Christians of varying denominations, charismatic and non-charismatic, Calvinist, Arminian, Wesleyan, Catholic and Protestant. I believe that what I am about the share is in full agreement with the Bible and United Methodist beliefs. So here are my conclusions on the subject. The key authority on the subject is the Bible. Specifically 1 Corinthians 12, Romans 12, Ephesians 4, 1 Peter 4, and various other New Testament references.

1). The Gifts represent an added dimension to the human experience. Scholars tell us that the Greek word for gift is "charisma" meaning "grace gift" or an underserved or free gift. Therefore spiritual gifts are not natural talents, like the ability to play the piano, or the ability to draw, or learned skills like woodworking or computer programming. But rather are empowerments of the Holy Spirit. They are given individually to members of the body of Christ as God wills through the Holy Spirit.

2).The gifts are given for the specific purpose of building unity within the body of Christ, the church. The Bible teaches that the gifts are

Chapter Four Serving

given to build harmony in the Christian movement so that together the church can do the work of ministry. The apostle Paul is clear that no one gift is more important than another, but that gifts work together for the purpose of making the church strong for its mission to the world. Ultimately the gifts prepare us for the great commission of making disciples for the transformation of the world.

3). Every Christian has at least one spiritual gift and most likely has several. It is estimated that about 75% of Christians know about spiritual gifts, but many do not actually know their own gifts. Without encouragement, it seems to me, that the majority of Christians may unknowingly neglect to identify and use these special endowments.

4). Some gifts reflect the normal activities of all Christians. For example all Christians are called to practice evangelism (witnessing), and giving. But only some Christians have the spiritual gift of evangelism or giving. Unfortunately statistics show that only about 1% of Christians believe they have the gift of evangelism. This may account for the decline of the church in our times. Most certainly more than 1% of Christians have this gift!

5). Spiritual gifts are not the ultimate consideration in Christian living. The apostle Paul follows 1 Corinthians chapter 12 with the love chapter of the Bible 1 Corinthians chapter 13. He says in no uncertain terms that we may have all the spiritual gifts in the world but if we do not have love we are nothing. This brings up the topic of the fruit of the spirit. The fruit of the spirit is a cluster of nine personal characteristics of the Christian attitude expressed as, "love, joy, peace, patience, kindness, goodness, faithfulness, gentleness, and self-control". (Galations 5:22-23 RSV). To live under the influence of the Holy Spirit is to reflect not one or two of these but all of them. That is way they are referred to as the "fruit" (singular) not the "fruits" of the Spirit.

6). Spiritual gifts can change and grow. One Christian said to me the other day, "I may have the gift of teaching but at my age I no longer want to teach". Still the spiritual gift of teaching is present. Out of my spiritual gift as pastor, I suggested that this individual could still be available to mentor other gifted teachers. Other Christians have shared with me that with experience their spiritual gift of administration, serving, helping, teaching, showing mercy has grown more focused and more intense over the years.

7). Use it or lose it! It is possible for spiritual gifts to be muted or weakened through lack of use. This is why it is so important to stay connected to the body of Christ through regular small group participation and corporate worship. Through these experiences spiritual gifts are encouraged and strengthened and used!

8). Some spiritual gifts can be very controversial! For this reason I have limited the list of spiritual gifts in my writings to 15 that are more commonly recognized and used in the majority of churches. These include the gifts of administration, evangelism, exhortation, faith, giving, healing, helps, knowledge, leadership, mercy, prophecy, service, Sheppard, teaching, wisdom.

Discussion Questions:

1). What hope for your spiritual life and the life of our church do you see in the use of our spiritual gifts?
2). What doubts or questions do you still have about spiritual gifts?

Memory Verse:

"As each has received a gift, employ it for one another, as good stewards of God's varied grace" (1 Peter 4:10 RSV).

Spiritual Gifts and Your Personal Mission -TLC Lesson 28

We all have heard about the topic of spiritual gifts. Also we have heard about the topic of personal mission statements. A logical next step is to ask the question, "How do my spiritual gifts fit with my personal mission?" To even ask this question is to declare that you have decided on very specific life path, a life path of Christian discipleship.

1). The Life Decision. The Bible says, "Therefore, if anyone is in Christ, he is a new creation; the old has passed away, behold, the new has come". (2 Corinthians 5:17 RSV). A hymn says, "I have decided to follow Jesus, no turning back, no turning back!"

Chapter Four Serving

To respond to Jesus Christ in this way is to be born again, filled with the fruit of the Holy Spirit, and empowered with the gifts of the Holy Spirit to be on a mission for God. This involves far more than just "joining church." This involves a life decision related to the question, "what does God want me to do with my life?" This is a question on the same level as the questions, "who should I marry and what will be my life work?" The bible teaches that every human being has spiritual gifts and a mission for God that must be accepted through a personal life decision.

2). The Meaning of Mission. A mission is defined as an important task or duty that is assigned, or self-imposed. Also a mission is an important goal or purpose that is accompanied by strong conviction or is considered a calling. Unlike some secular thinking that says only ordained clergy are called and spiritually gifted, the Bible teaches that all Christians are called and gifted for ministry. Therefore all Christians have a God ordained "life mission". So the question for each of us is this, "what does God want me to do with my life?" Pastor Rick Warren calls this, "The Purpose Driven Life!" Our mission is assigned by God but must also be self-imposed to be fulfilled.

3). The Elements of Full Discipleship. In the secular world anyone who says they believe in Jesus is considered a disciple. From a biblical perspective a disciple is a disciplined follower of Jesus who is involved in a more detailed life path involving numerous elements. When I think about "full discipleship" at least five elements come to mind.

A). Talents. Simply defined, talents are God given "natural abilities". A talent may also be defined as a special ability that allows someone to do something very well. We think of people who have a natural athletic ability, a mathematical ability, and artistic ability, an ability to play chess, or numerous other abilities. Talents may or may not be used for spiritual benefit. The talented person must make a decision as to how to apply their talent in a spiritual way.

B). Spiritual Gifts. Simply defined, Spiritual Gifts are God given "supernatural abilities" given for the purpose of spiritual ministry.

TLC Groups for Busy Disciples

The spiritually gifted person can only decide either to use these gifts or not to use them. They cannot be used in an unspiritual way (as can talents) but must be used in a spiritual way if they are used at all. The Bible lists 27 spiritual gifts, depending on Interpretation. For the purposes of this teaching I have included 15 gifts, Administration, Evangelism, Exhortation, Faith, Giving, Healing, Helps, Knowledge, Leadership, Mercy, Prophecy, Service, Shepherd, Teaching, and Wisdom.

C). Core Values. Core values are the guiding principles, bedrock beliefs, or deep convictions that determine behavior and action. Some examples of core values are belief God, belief that family is of fundamental importance, belief that honesty is always the best policy, belief in serving others, etc.

D). Passions. A passion is a strong feeling of enthusiasm or excitement for something or about doing something. Christians can be said to have a passion for prayer, for children's ministry, for youth ministry, for preaching, for teaching, for leading and or many other types of ministry.

E). Goals. A goal is a desired result that a person envisions, plans and commits to achieve. For example, "will I use my talent for singing and my spiritual gift for evangelism by singing in the church choir this year, or I will use my passion for youth ministry and my spiritual gift of teaching by signing up to teach the 7th grade class this year". Full discipleship brings together talents, spiritual gifts, core values, passions, and goals in an integrated commitment to be employed in the work of Jesus' kingdom.

Discussion Questions:

1). How have you experienced the coming together of you talents, spiritual gifts, core values, passions, mission, and goals in Christian service?
2). How can we as a church help others to experience full discipleship?

Memory Verse:

Chapter Four Serving

"Now you are the body of Christ and individually members of it". (1 Corinthians 12:27 RSV).

You Were Made For a Mission - TLC Lesson 29

Why are we here? This is an age-old question asked by theologians, philosophers, and scientists for centuries. Someone has asked, isn't there more to life than to, "eat, drink, and be merry for tomorrow we die?" The same person answered the question by saying, "probably not if there is no creator". This gives rise to another age-old question, "does God exist?"

"The great thing about Rick Warren's book, "The Purpose Driven Life", is that it starts out with the opening sentence: "It's not about you." He goes on to say, "The purpose of your life is far greater than your own personal fulfillment, your peace of mind, or even your happiness. It's far greater than your family, your career, or even your wildest dreams and ambitions. If you want to know why you were placed on this planet, you must begin with God. You were born by his purpose and for his purpose."[42]

So let us begin with God! TLC groups are founded on the premise that all people are called by God, through Jesus Christ, to be loyal to God's church through prayers, presence, gifts, service, and witness. So my question for this TLC lesson is, "not do you have a mission, but what is your mission?" Even more to the point is a takeoff on the old "Mission Impossible" statement, "should you choose to accept this mission you will find your instructions in the following pages which will not self destruct!" Pages of the Bible that is!

Jesus had a Mission. "The Spirit of the Lord is upon me, because he has anointed me to preach good news to the poor. He has sent me to proclaim release to the captives and recovering of sight to the blind, to set at liberty those who are oppressed, to proclaim the acceptable year of the Lord". (Luke 4:18-19 RSV). Jesus' mission was salvation for the whole world.

Jesus' Mission is Our Mission. Jesus said to his disciples, "Peace is with you. As the Father has sent me, even so I send you." (John

TLC Groups for Busy Disciples

20:21 RSV). And Jesus came and said to them, "All authority in heaven and on earth has been given to me. Go therefore and make disciples of all nations, baptizing them in the name of the Father and of the Son and of the Holy Spirit, teaching them to observe all that I have commanded you; and lo, I am with you always, to the close of the age." (Matthew 28:18-20 RSV). As Christians our mission is to "make disciples for the transformation of the world". As individuals we are called to define our personal mission based on our Spiritual Gifts, talents, core values, passions and goals.

You can know your mission! Some years ago Dr. Findley B. Edge wrote a book entitled, "The Greening of the Church".[43] in this book he said that when you find your mission for Jesus three things will happen in your life.

1). <u>You will shout eureka!</u> In other words this will be an A Ha moment for you. Your passion for this mission will be extremely strong.

2). <u>You will dream dreams about your mission</u>. This means "day dreams". You will be constantly thinking up ways to fulfill your mission.

3). <u>You will talk, talk, and talk about your mission</u>. You will be constantly sharing your dream with your family members, church members and anyone who will listen.

<u>Discussion Questions</u>:

1). When was a there time in your life that you just had to talk about your mission all the time?
2). What is Jesus calling you to do for him now?

<u>Memory Verse</u>:

"Peace is with you. As the Father has sent me, even so I send you." (John 20:21 RSV).

The Elements of a Mission Statement – TLC Lesson 30

Chapter Four Serving

We all have a mission. We learned in TLC lesson number 29 that all Christians have a God ordained "life mission". So the question for each of us is this, "what does God want us to do with our lives?" Our mission is given by God but must also be self-imposed in order to be fulfilled.

Jesus Had a Mission."The Spirit of the Lord is upon me, because he has anointed me to preach good news to the poor. He has sent me to proclaim release to the captives and recovering of sight to the blind, to set at liberty those who are oppressed, to proclaim the acceptable year of the Lord". (Luke 4:18-19 RSV). Jesus' mission was to bring salvation to the whole world.

Mission statements are very common.. Twenty first century Christians and churches often write their life missions down in the form of statements that clarify for the world exactly that they feel called to do for God. For example the mission statement of the United Methodist Church is "to make disciples of Jesus Christ for the transformation of the world".

Mission statements involve more than just a sentence. While the best mission statements are twenty five words or less written in one sentence that an eight year old child can understand, such statements involve certain elements or characteristics that give them true eternal substance.

Elements of a mission statement:

- A one sentence, clear, concise statement that says who we are, what we do, and for whom.

- Some form of disciple making.

- A specific task that a person or persons are sent to perform" (Webster).
- A short, generalized statement based on "core values" and made real through "vision".

- Twenty five words or less that can be quickly and easily memorized.

TLC Groups for Busy Disciples

- Understood by and eight year old.

- Should be written down, memorized, and constantly repeated in each other's presence.
- It is more important to be in mission than to have a mission statement!

Mission Statements are always based on "Core Values" Core values are:

- Our deepest convictions or bedrock beliefs.
- A fundamental set of guiding principles.
- The foundation upon which "Mission" and "Vision" are built.
- The glue that binds us together.
- Should be written down, memorized, and constantly repeated in each other's presence.

Mission Statements are brought to life through "Vision Statements".

Vision statements are:

- Statements that explain "how" you will carry out your mission in more specific details.
- A "plan" with a focus, timeline, beginning and ending times.

- A paragraph that expands and explains the one sentence "mission statement".
- Vision leads to goals and goal setting and needs follow-up! In TLC Lesson 31 we will all write a personal mission statement.

Discussion Questions:

1). Have you ever written a personal mission statement as a disciple?
2). What do you think a personal mission statement should say?

Memory Verse:

Chapter Four Serving

"The Spirit of the Lord is upon me, because he has anointed me to preach good news to the poor. He has sent me to proclaim release to the captives and recovering of sight to the blind, to set at liberty those who are oppressed, to proclaim the acceptable year of the Lord". (Luke 4:18-19 RSV).

Writing Your Personal Mission Statement – TLC lesson 31

We learned in TLC lesson number 29 that all Christians have a God ordained "life mission". The question for each of us is this, "what does God want us to do with our lives?" Our mission is given by God but must also be self-imposed in order to be fulfilled. The best mission statements are 25 words or less written in one sentence that an eight-year-old child can understand. A mission statement contains the elements of normal sentence construction and can be broken down into:

Subject
      Possessive pronoun -   My
      Noun -   mission
Predicate
      Linking Verb -   is
      Preposition -   to
      Verb   equip   how do you want to help?
      Article -   the
      Object noun -   saints   who do you want to help?
      Conjunction -   for
      Article -   the
      Adjective -   work
      Preposition -   of
      Noun-   ministry what do you want to help them do?

An example of a mission statement is, "My mission is to train (how) millennial adults (who) to lead youth groups (what)".

Another example of a mission statement is, "My mission is to teach (how) women (who) how to study the Bible (what)."

You can write your personal mission statement by prayerfully searching your heart and filling in the blanks below.

TLC Groups for Busy Disciples

How do you want to help? Write down a verb that describes how you feel called to help.

My **verb** is:_____

Who do you want to help? Write down a people group that you feel called to help.

My **who** is _____

What do you want to help them do? Write down some ideas about what you feel called to help others do.

My **what** is _____

Put it all together by placing the above verb, who and what into the following sentence.

My mission is to _____, with _____

to _____ .

Discussion Question:

Go around the room and have each person in the group share their mission statement. Give time for the group to comment on each other's mission statement.

Memory Verse:

"Go therefore and make disciples of all nations, baptizing them in the name of the father and of the son and of the Holy Spirit." (Matthew 28:19 RSV).

What a Mission Statement Is Not! TLC Lesson 32

In TLC lesson 30 we talked about the elements of a mission statement. A brief review of that lesson will remind us that these elements include:

Chapter Four Serving

- A one sentence, clear, concise statement that says who we are, what we do, and for whom.
- Some form of disciple making.

- A specific task that a person or persons are sent to perform" (Webster).

- A short, generalized statement based on "core values" and made real through "vision".
- Twenty five words or less that can be quickly and easily memorized.
- Understood by and eight year old.

- Should be written down, memorized, and constantly repeated in each other's presence.
- It is more important to be in mission than to have a mission statement!

As we continue to develop our personal mission statements we often encounter misunderstandings and confusion about what really qualifies as a mission statement. One way to help clarify our understanding of mission statements is to make a list of "what a mission statement is not".
A mission statement is not:

1). A job description. A job description is an outline of your daily activities that relate to your occupation. The day will come when you will retire from your job and you will no longer need a job description. A mission statement is a declaration and description of your God given calling and your passion for ministry. You will never retire from this, although your involvement will most likely decline with the years. Christians normally transition from active mission to a mentoring role as they become the respected "elders" of the church.

2). A Role. A role is a relationship accepted by you in response to your life circumstances. For a period of time you may be the parent of a toddler. The day will come when you are no longer caring for a toddler and your role will change. Welcome to the teen years! Our roles in life change with circumstances and we accept (or try to reject) this role change. Such is life. Sometimes society, family, the church, or community organizations can thrust a role upon us even when we don't want that role. Our mission does not change. Our mission is not thrust upon us by others or by God. Our mission is fueled by our own passion and is joyfully accepted as that which fulfills and completes us.

3). <u>A To Do List</u>. A to do list is an organizational time saver or a nightmare depending on how long and/or how complicated the list. My to do list has kept me on track and on time for most of my life. For most of my life I have tried to shorten the list. When I retired I tried to live without a to do list only to discover that to be impossible. The greater my memory loss the greater my need for a list. A mission statement is not a list but a joy. I like to dream about my mission. I like to forget my to do list! In heaven there will be no lists but there will be mission.

4). <u>A Vision Statement</u>. A vision statement is a detailed "how to" list of how you will carry out your mission. A mission statement is one sentence. A vision statement is a paragraph or more. A mission statement is a general statement of what you will do for Jesus (i.e. make disciples). A vision statement is a more detailed statement of "how" you will make disciples (i.e. Connect, Grow, Serve through goal setting, planning, evaluating, redirecting, hard work, team work, etc.).

Discussion Questions:

1). Share with the group how you find joy in doing your mission.
2). Share with the group how you have fulfilled your mission through the vision of your local church.

Memory Verse:

"For I know the plans I have for you, says the Lord, plans for welfare and not for evil, to give you a future and a hope". (Jeremiah 29:11 RSV).

Chapter Four Serving

Team Ministry - TLC Lesson 33

The Bible tells us that as the early church grew they organized themselves for ministry. Acts chapter 6 records the dedication of the first deacons who were commissioned to care for widows. (Acts 6:1-7 RSV). Before his conversion, Paul persecuted the followers of Jesus. The first disciples of Jesus became known as "followers of the Way". (Acts 9:1-2 RSV). The Apostle Paul later described the emerging church as a body with various parts but with one purpose, to build each other up into a unity that would show to the world the "way" of Jesus. (1 Corinthians 12:4-7 RSV).

Jesus gave his disciples a great commission to go into all the world and make disciples of every nation. (Matthew 28:18-28 RSV). As history unfolded, the church became organized in order to carry out the mission of Jesus. Deacons and elders emerged. Local churches emerged in communities from Jerusalem to Rome. Local Christians used their spiritual gifts to work as the Body of Christ to spread the Gospel. Ministry was not limited to the apostles but was embraced as a team effort.

The modern day church is patterned after the early church. While there are many denominations and varying structures and polities, the church of today is basically a band of believers who seek to use their spiritual gifts to help people become "followers of the Way". At best the church is a "simple church", with mean lean organizational structures, that facilitate the ministry of all Christians as a team! Team ministry has some very powerful and helpful elements.

1). **Pastors** are called to be "leaders" who equip the saints (all Christians) for the work of ministry. Pastors are not called to do the entire ministry, but to mobilize the church for team ministry. (Ephesians 4:11-12 RSV).

2). **Laity** are called and gifted by the Holy Spirit to do ministry. Every Christian is a minister. Unfortunately in the modern day church we often fail to understand this concept. The fact remains that Jesus wants every Christian to be in ministry. (Romans 12, Ephesians 4, I Corinthians 12 RSV).

TLC Groups for Busy Disciples

3). **Spiritual Formation** happens through team ministry as individuals hold each other accountable for ministry, pray for one another, study together, train together, forgive one another, and train others for ministry. (Galatians 5:22-26).

4). **Koinonia** develops within the church through team ministry. The word Koinonia appears 19 times the New Testament. It is translated "fellowship" twelve times, "sharing" three times, and "participation" and "contribution" twice each. (Acts 2:42-47 RSV).

5). **More is Accomplished** through team ministry as:

- People's potential is unlocked.
- New Ideas are shared and tried.
- Permission to fail is given.
- Creative disagreement is encouraged and accepted.
- Members really listen to each other.
- Hidden agendas are eliminated.
- A family of faith emerges.
- Volunteerism grows because of the witness of the team.

Discussion Questions:

1). How do you think we are doing as a church in regard to team Ministry?
2). What do you think can be done to increase team ministry in our church?

Memory Verse:

"For as in one body we have many members, and all the members do not have the same function, so we, though many, are one body in Christ, and individually members one of another". (Romans 12:4 RSV).

Chapter Five Giving

TLC Groups for Busy Disciples

~ Chapter Five - Giving ~

Chapter Five Giving

The Sermon on the Amount - TLC Lesson 34

The TLC group lessons are based on the membership commitment of the local church formed around praying, witnessing, worshipping, serving and giving. In this lesson we turn our attention to the topic of giving. When we speak of giving we are thinking of financial giving. The topic of spiritual gifts is dealt with under the membership vow of serving, so when we speak of giving in this context we are talking about financial stewardship. The title of this lesson is taken from the book written by pastor Brian K Bauknight entitled, "Right on The Money, Messages for Spiritual Growth through Giving". Chapter ten of his book is entitled, "Sermon on The Amount".[44]

Dr. Bauknight takes for his text 2 Corinthians 9:7 which says, "Everyone must make up his own mind as to how much he should give. Don't force anyone to give more than he really wants to, for cheerful givers are the ones God prizes". (2 Corinthians 9:7 Living Bible).

The essence of his message is personal choice. Each person must decide. The church should not dictate, but the church can help with this decision. The church can and should nurture a giving life style. Dr. Bauknight gives three considerations as to how a Christian can make this decision.

1). <u>Lean into the Spirit of God</u>.[45] He says, "The church is about faith rising not fund raising"[46]. We pray and ask God what we should give and we listen to the Holy Spirit's answer. In the end, giving is a matter of the heart. Each of us must give according to our deepest convictions.

2). <u>The Principle of Proportionality</u>.[47] The idea here is that we give a portion of income, not just a dollar amount. A farmer in a church where I served asked me, "What should I base my giving on?" I said, "Your income". He said, "I am self employed, what should I do?" I said, "Do you pay income taxes?" He said, "Yes". I said, "go to the line on your tax form that says 'figure your tax on this' and also figure your giving on this amount. Decide what proportion of your taxable income you will give. According to records the average annual giving in American Churches is about 2.5% of that line.

TLC Groups for Busy Disciples

Some Christians believe in the tithe and give 10% of that line. Others give even more. The spiritual challenge is to decide in your heart, with God's help, what you will give. I know from experience that if the local church were to give an average of 3% to 4% there would be no money problems in the church. Imagine what the church could do if the average were 10%.

3). <u>The Principle of Tithing</u>.[48] According to the Old Testament the tithe is required by law. (Malachi 3:8-10). There are tithes, which belong to God, and there are offerings which are free will gifts beyond the tithe. The New Testament does not make tithing a law but assumes the principle. Therefore the ultimate goal of our proportional giving is the tithe. In his book, <u>The Disciple's Path</u>, pastor James A. Harnish describes the Christian life as a journey or a path. We move along this path from exploring to getting started, to going deeper, to centering. In regard to financial giving we move from occasional giving, to regular giving, to tithing, to sacrificial generosity beyond the tithe.[49] the challenge before us is to grow in our giving. If we are at 1% could we move to 2%. If we are at 4% could we move to 5%? Could we ultimately move to the tithe?

Discussion Questions:

1. How do you feel about the principle of the tithe?
2. How do you feel about the way our church teaches stewardship?

Memory Verse:

"Everyone must make up his own mind as to how much he should give. Don't force anyone to give more than he really wants to, for cheerful givers are the ones God prizes". (2 Corinthians 9:7 Living Bible).

Tithes and Offerings - TLC Lesson 35

Over the years I have used a specific phrase in morning worship during the time of the morning offering. I have said, "let us worship the Lord with the giving of his tithes and our offerings". I have gotten used to this common phrase and I hunch so has my congregation. It would be all too easy to think of tithes and offerings as basically the same thing. However in the back of my mind there is a distinction, a distinction that

Chapter Five Giving

we as disciples often miss. Biblically speaking, the tithe is a one-tenth part of something, paid as a contribution. In the Old Testament the tithe was considered a Law and the people were expected to give this amount to the Lord. The Law covered many aspects for living, including care of the Levite priests, release from debt, and caring for the poor. Technically speaking, the New Testament does not make tithing a law but does extend the spirit of the tithe. Jesus corrected the religious leaders of the day by saying, "But woe to you Pharisees! For you tithe mint and rue and every herb, and neglect justice and the love of God; these you ought to have done, without neglecting the others". (Luke 11:42 RSV).Giving in the Christian frame of reference basically involves three things, the tithe, designated offerings, and free will offerings.

1). Tithes represent a proportioned amount given to support the work of the church in all of its aspects including the operating budget, mission outreach, support of pastors and staff, building maintenance and all other expenses. Most churches have an annual stewardship campaign, including stewardship sermons, to raise this support. The outcome is an estimated total giving amount upon which the church can base its budget for the coming year. People are asked to complete a pledge card on which they tell the church how much the church can expect for its support. People often ask, "how should I determine how much to give?" The answer to that question is, "give proportionally". Giving proportionally involves prayerfully looking at one's yearly family income and deciding what percentage of that income one will pledge to the church. The New Testament gives good advice in the following words, "each one must do as he has made up his mind, not reluctantly or under compulsion, for God loves a cheerful giver". (2 Corinthians 9:7 RSV). The actual facts, according to researchers, reveal the following information.

- About 3 to 5 percent of Christians give 10% or more (tithe).
- The average household giving is about 2.5% for all denominations with some giving less and others more.
- The average weekly giving is about $17.

- People who tithe typically have less debt and 28% are debt free.

- If a congregation can encourage the averaging giving to be 3% to 4% the church would have no financial problems at all.

TLC Groups for Busy Disciples

-   If the church tithed, (10%), the church could have miraculous ministry potential.

2). Designated Offerings are different from tithes in that they are not based on a percentage of income. They are special offerings through which Christians are invited to support causes sponsored by their church or denomination. The United Methodist Church, for example, has six annual special offerings designated for "Human Relations", "UMCOR", "Native American Ministries", "Peace with Justice", "World Communion", and "Student Day".

3). Free Will Offerings are voluntary offerings made in addition to what is required by a pledge or a designated offering. Local churches often receive special offerings to support missionaries, mission trips, college student ministries, music ministries, and any number of special outreach projects envisioned by the local church.

Discussion Questions:

1. What questions do you have about the various kinds of giving practiced by your church?
2. What do you believe could be done to increase giving to your local church?

Memory Verse:

"Bring the full tithes into the storehouse, that there may be food in my house; and thereby put me to the test, says the Lord of hosts, if I will not open the windows of heaven for you and pour down for you an overflowing blessing". (Malachi 3:10 RSV)

Growth in Giving - TLC Lesson 36

When we join the church we make a covenant with God and each other to participate in its ministries by our prayers, presence, gifts, service, and witness. A vital part of that covenant is our commitment to grow in these areas of discipleship. Growth in giving is a vital part of that covenant. We ask ourselves, how can I give more? The church leadership asks, how can we encourage growth in giving? Here are 10 suggestions to help answer these questions.

Chapter Five Giving

1). <u>Pray</u>. The bible gives clear instruction on how to approach giving. "Each one must do as he has made up his mind, not reluctantly or under compulsion, for God loves a cheerful giver". (2 Corinthians 9:7 RSV). The ultimate answer as to how much we should give is summed up in this, "continually ask God, through prayer, how you should give and make giving a spiritual formation process."

2). <u>Keep a Positive Attitude</u>. Try not to base your giving on your changing analysis of how the church is doing. Don't limit your giving based on your disagreement with the current church budget or goals. Focus instead on your personal stewardship by giving according to what God wants from you. Growth in giving is more about faith rising than fund raising!

3). <u>Focus on Ministry Not Numbers.</u> Try to view your giving by looking at the ministry the church is doing without being critical of the cost. Do the best you can and trust the rest to others as God leads them.

4). <u>Do an Estimate of Giving Card</u>. Members who fill out an annual pledge card during the church stewardship emphasis tend to grow in their giving.

5). <u>Use Offering Envelopes Mailed to Your Home</u>. Statistics show that total church giving increases by about 10% just by mailing out offering envelopes rather than not using them or having them picked up at church.

6). <u>Ongoing Stewardship Study</u>. Courses offered by the local church, such as David Ramsey's "Financial Peace University", help Christians learn how to create a budget, save money, get out of debt, make a plan for spending and learn to give more to God. This is a true win/win opportunity.

7). <u>Listen to Stewardship Testimonies</u>. Vital Local churches give opportunities for members to give testimonies during worship services about how they are growing in prayers, presence, gifts, service and witness.

TLC Groups for Busy Disciples

8). <u>Have a Clear Vision of Your Church's Ministry</u>. Ask the church office for a print out of the church's mission statement, core values, vision statement and current goals. The more excited about what your church is doing the more excited you will be about giving.

9). <u>Try Online Giving</u>. Most churches now offer the opportunity to give through automatic withdrawal of a designated amount of your choosing. This is a great way to remain consistent in your giving.

10). <u>Try to Out Give God</u>. The Bible says, "Bring the full tithes into the storehouse, that there may be food in my house; and thereby put me to the test, says the Lord of hosts, if I will not open the windows of heaven for you and pour down for you an overflowing blessing". (Malachi 3:10 RSV). A pastor once challenged his congregation with these words, "try tithing for one month and if God does not bless you, we will give the money back!" It would be interesting for the members of our church to try this!

Discussion Questions:

1. Which of the above suggestions would most help you, why?
2. Which of the above suggestions would be the most challenging for you? Why?

Memory Verse:

"Do not lay up for yourselves treasures on earth, where moth and rust consume and where thieves break in and steal, but lay up for you treasures in heaven, where neither moth nor rust consumes and where thieves do not break in and steal. For where your treasure is, there will your heart be also". Matthew 6:19-21)

~ Chapter Six
Understanding Scripture ~

TLC Groups for Busy Disciples

Twenty Three Minutes A Day - TLC Lesson 37

Someone once asked me, "How long would it take to read the entire Bible through?" Having been asked this question before, I responded, "23 minutes a day or 85 hours a year for the King James Version". Some versions might take a little longer depending on the translation. Recently, using the Bible Gateway[1] audio Bible I timed the reading of the Bible in the King James Version. It came out to 6.5 minutes per page. Multiplied by 814 pages for the old and New Testaments this came out to a total of 85 hours or 23 minutes a day for a year. I once attended a freshman seminary class in which the professor asked the question, "How many in today's class have ever read the entire Bible through? There were 200 students in the class. Three students held up their hands. The rest were, to say the least, shocked. If future pastors have not read the Bible through, where does this leave the laity? There is real value to reading the Bible through once per year. You can do it in 23 minutes per day. If you prefer a two year schedule, you can do it in 12 minutes per day. So why would anyone do this? Here is a list of good reasons.

1). It Will Show You the Way of Salvation. "For by grace you have been saved through faith; and this is not your own doing, it is the gift of God not because of works, lest any man should boast" (Ephesians 2:8-9 RSV) "Jesus answered him, "Truly, truly, I say to you, unless one is born anew, he cannot see the kingdom of God." (John 3:3 RSV). "For God so loved the world that he gave his only Son, that whoever believes in him should not perish but have eternal life". (John 3:16 RSV). "If you confess with your lips that Jesus is Lord and believe in your heart that God raised him from the dead, you will be saved. For man believes with his heart and so is justified, and he confesses with his lips and so is saved". (Romans 10:9-10 RSV).

2). It Will Lead You to the Forgiveness of Sins   "If we confess our sins, he is faithful and just and will forgive us our sins and purify us from all unrighteousness". (1 John 1:9 RSV).

3). It Will Help You Overcome Temptation. "And the tempter came and said to him, "If you are the Son of God, command these stones

Chapter Six Understanding Scripture

to become loaves of bread." But he answered, "It is written, 'Man shall not live by bread alone, but by every word that proceeds from the mouth of God'". (Matthew 4:3-4 RSV)

4). It Will Bring Spiritual Maturity. "But the fruit of the Spirit is love, joy, peace, patience, kindness, goodness, faithfulness, gentleness, self-control; against such there is no law. And those who belong to Christ Jesus have crucified the flesh with its passions and desires". (Galations 5:22-24 RSV).

5). It Will Help You Find God's Will for Your Life. "We know that in everything God works for good with those who love him, who are called according to his purpose". (Romans 8:28 RSV).

6). It Will Help You Through Difficult Times. "The Lord is my shepherd, I shall not want; he makes me lie down in green pastures He leads me beside still waters; he restores my soul". (Psalm 23:1-3 RSV).

7). It Will Guide You into A Life of Holiness. "I have laid up thy word in my heart that I might not sin against thee". (Psalm 119:11 RSV).
Getting Started. Select a modern version you like. Begin with Genesis and read four pages per day. The New Revised Standard Version (NRSV) is a good selection. Go on line to Biblegateway.com. Select "Audio Bible" and beginning with Genesis listen as the entire Bible is read for you in a version of your choosing.[50] this is a great way to learn how to pronounce those big names!

Discussion Questions:

1. How challenging would it be for you to read the Bible through in a year? Why.
2. What benefits do you see in reading the Bible through in a year?

Memory Verse:

"Your word is a lamp to my feet and a light to my path". (Psalm 119:105 RSV)

TLC Groups for Busy Disciples

How to Memorize Scripture - TLC Lesson 38

When I was a young Christian, one of my spiritual mentors suggested that I try memorizing Scripture. He quoted Psalm 119 and told me that this would be a great way to start out on my discipleship journey. He was right! I have never regretted the time I have spent memorizing scripture. The Bible says, "How can a young man keep his way pure? By living by Your Word. I have looked for you with all my heart. Do not let me turn from Your Law. Your Word have I hid in my heart, that I may not sin against you" (Psalm 119:9-11 NLV). So why should we memorize scripture?

Why Memorize Bible Verses?

Here are several good reasons.

1). It Helps You to Know God and Jesus Christ. Research tells us that the majority of human beings believe in God in some way, but many are unclear about who God and Jesus really are. It has been said that the Bible is His-Story. Memorizing verses that describe the nature and characteristics of God and Christ will help you form a deeper understanding of and relationship with God. Take John 3:16 for example. You can learn a lot about God and Jesus by simply studying this verse in depth.

2). It Will Give You Guidance For Making Life Decisions. The Bible says, "Trust in the Lord with all your heart, and do not rely on your own insight. In all your ways acknowledge him and he will make straight your paths". (Proverbs 3:5-6 RSV). There is an old phrase that many Christians have used to help guide them through life, "what would Jesus do?" Memorizing scripture verses about Jesus' teaching is a good way to apply this saying.

3). It Will Help You Overcome Temptation. The Bible says, "No temptation has overtaken you that are not common to man. God is faithful, and he will not let you be tempted beyond your strength, but with the temptation will also provide the way of escape, that you may be able to endure it". (1 Corinthians 10:13 RSV).

Chapter Six Understanding Scripture

4). <u>It Will Give You Words To Share Your Faith</u>. The Bible says, "Always be prepared to make a defense to anyone who calls you to account for the hope that is in you, yet do it with gentleness and reverence". (1 Peter 3:15 RSV). If someone asks you what you believe, it always helps to have a verse or two on hand to share.

How to Memorize Scripture.

1). <u>Select A Version of The Bible That Is Easy To Understand</u>. A good suggestion is the New Revised Standard Version (NRSV). Stick with one version. It is easier to memorize one version of verses than to try to memorize multiple translations.

2). <u>Write Verses Down On Small Cards</u>. You can do this by hand or you can purchase Bible memory verse packets from publishers like The Navagators.[51] You can also register on line to receive a "verse of the day" from Bible Gateway.[52]

3). <u>Select Verses by Themes</u>. Do a Google search to find Bible verses related to major spiritual themes. For example, "what does the Bible say about forgiveness, temptation, sin, salvation, peace, heaven, Jesus, God, The Holy Spirit, healing, hope, spiritual gifts, the fruit of the spirit, etc.

4). <u>Use Casual Reading as Your Method</u>. It is better to carry memory cards with you and casually read over them at breakfast, lunch, supper and bedtime rather than to try to force feed your memory with intensive multiple repetitive reading. Over time the verses will become a part of you and memory will come naturally.

5). <u>Post A Verse of the Day on your Refrigerator or Mirror</u>. Casually look at it whenever you go to the fridge or stand in front of the mirror.

Discussion Questions:

1. How do you think memorizing scripture can be of benefit to you?
2. What might hinder you from memorizing scripture?

Memory Verse:

TLC Groups for Busy Disciples

"Indeed, the word of God is living and active, sharper than any two-edged sword, piercing until it divides soul from spirit, joints from marrow; it is able to judge the thoughts and intentions of the heart". (Hebrews 4:12) NRSV).

The Books of the Bible - TLC Lesson 39

One of the first things I can remember doing in Sunday school was memorizing the 66 books of the Bible. Over the years there have been times when I took time to review that memory work. The benefit of knowing the names of these books is that it gives one a broad understanding of what the Bible contains. Another helpful list to memorize is a chronological list of Biblical history as presented in the 39 books of the Old Testament and the 27 books of the New Testament. Following are two such listings.

The Old Testament (39 Books).

> **The Pentateuch**. (5) Genesis, Exodus, Leviticus, Numbers, and Deuteronomy.
> **The Historical Books**. (12) Joshua, Judges, Ruth, 1&2 Samuel, 1&2 Kings, 1&2 Chronicles, Ezra, Nehemiah, and Esther.
> **Poetic and Wisdom Books**. (5) Job, Psalms, Proverbs, Ecclesiastes, Song of Solomon.
> **Major Prophets**. (5) Isaiah, Jeremiah, Lamentations, Ezekiel, and Daniel.
> **Minor Prophets.** (12) Hosea, Joel, Amos, Obadiah, Jonah, Micah, Nahum, Habakkuk, Zephaniah, Haggai, Zechariah, and Malachi.

The New Testament (27 books).

> **The Gospels.** (4) Matthew, Mark, Luke, and John).
> **Acts of the Apostles.** (1).
> **General Epistles.** (7) James, 2 & 2 Peter, 1,2, & 3 John, Jude.
> **Paul's Epistles.** (9) Romans, 1 & 2 Corinthians, Galatians, Ephesians, Philippians, Colossians. 1 & 2 Thessalonians.
> **Hebrews.** (1).

Chapter Six Understanding Scripture

Pastoral Epistles. (4) 1 & 2 Timothy, Titus, Philemon.
Revelation. (1).

General Topics Covered.

My purpose here is to give a brief overview of topics covered in the Bible, not to debate the historicity or the theological interpretations these topics. Some of these dates will be disputed by scholars. There is general agreement on the dates of the Assyrian Captivity, 722 B.C. and the Babylonian Captivity, 586 B.C. while other dates may be in question.

Creation to Abraham. (13.77 billion to 2000 (B.C.). I have included a reconciliatory view of science and scripture in these dates to show that the Bible and modern science are not in conflict, as some may contend.[53] Genesis 1:1-11.

Abraham to Moses (2000 -1500 B.C.). The stories of Abraham, Isaac, Jacob and Joseph and Egypt. Genesis 12-50.

The Exodus. (1500-1460 B.C.). Moses, Joshua, Canaan. Exodus, Leviticus, Numbers, Deuteronomy.

The Conquest of Canaan (1460 -1450 B.C.). The twelve tribes of Israel. Joshua.
The Period of the Judges (1450 –1102 B.C.). The books of Judges and Ruth.
The United Kingdom (1102 – 982 B.C.). Samuel, Saul, David, Solomon. Books of 1&2 Samuel, 1&2 Kings,1&2 Chronicles.
The Divided Kingdom (982-722 B.C.). Two kingdoms, Israel and Judah
The Kingdom of Judah (722-586 B.C.). The Assyrian Captivity 722 B.C.
The Captivity (586 – 538 B.C.). The Babylonian captivity. 586 B.C.
The Restoration (538-391 B.C.). The books of Ezra, Nehemiah, and Esther.
The Time between the Testaments (391-4 B.C.).

The Life of Christ (4 B.C. – 29 A.D.). The books of Matthew, Mark, Luke and John.

TLC Groups for Busy Disciples

The Spread of Christianity (29 – 100 A.D.). The book of acts and the Epistles.

Discussion Questions:

1. What is your favorite Bible story and why?
2. How has the Bible affected your life?

Memory Verse:

"In the beginning when God created the heavens and the earth" (Genesis 1:1 NRSV).

What the Bible Says About God - TLC Lesson 40

The Merriam-Webster Dictionary defines God as the supreme or ultimate reality: the Being perfect in power, wisdom, and goodness who is worshipped as creator and ruler of the universe.[54] The Free Dictionary defines God as a being conceived as the perfect, omnipotent, omniscient originator and ruler of the universe, the principal object of faith and worship in monotheistic religions.[55] It is impossible to summarize everything the Bible says about God in a one page TLC lesson. My purpose here is to give a general overview of the Christian understanding of God as described in the Old and New Testaments.

1). <u>God is a Personal Being</u>. The Bible portrays God as a being of eternal and spiritual attributes who seeks to be in relationship with the whole universe including all forms of life and especially human beings. To say that God is a personal being does not imply, as some would suggest, that God is in any way anthropomorphic. Neither does this mean that God is a creation of the human mind. Scripture portrays God as creating, speaking, expressing anger, forgiving, loving, guiding, answering prayer, and functioning in much the same way as humans except for the fact that the God of the Bible is eternal, unlimited, all powerful, all knowing, all loving, holy, unerring, and unique. God does not have a physical body or physical characteristics, though God is portrayed as seeing, hearing, knowing, acting, and interacting.
2). <u>God has Attributes</u>. The Bible describes God in numerous ways.

Chapter Six Understanding Scripture

Infinite. Boundless, endless, without end or limits. "I am the Alpha and the Omega," says the Lord God, who is and who was and who is to come, the Almighty". (Revelation 1:8 RSV).

Spiritual. "God is spirit, and those who worship him must worship in spirit and truth." (John 4:24 NRSV).

Omnipotent. All powerful and unlimited in authority. "Ah Lord GOD! It is you who made the heavens and the earth by your great power and by your outstretched arm! Nothing is too hard for you." (Jeremiah 32:17 NRSV).

Omnipresent. Present in all places at all times. "Where can I go from your spirit? Or where can I flee from you presence? If ascend to heaven, you are there; if I make my bed in Sheol, you are there. If I take the wings of the morning and settle at the farthest limits of the sea, even there your hand shall lead me, and your right hand shall hold me fast." (Psalm 139:7-10 NRSV).

Omniscient. All knowing, all wise, all seeing. "O Lord, you have searched me and known me. You know when I sit down and when I rise up; you discern my thoughts from far away. You search out my path and my lying down, and are acquainted with all my ways." (Psalm 139:1-3 NRSV).

Love. Unconditional acceptance and grace. "For God so loved the world that he gave his only Son, so that everyone who believes in him may not perish but may have eternal life." (John 3:16 NRSV).

Holy. Set apart, transcendent, sacred, separate, and totally other. "In the year that King Uzziah died, I saw the Lord sitting on a throne, high and lofty; and the hem of his robe filled the temple. Seraphs were in attendance above him; each had six wings: with two they covered their faces, and with two they covered their feet, and with two they flew. And one called to another and said: "Holy, holy, holy is the Lord of the whole earth is full of his glory." (Isaiah 6:1-3).

God Interacts With People.

Throughout the Bible God is portrayed as interacting with people. We think of Moses and the burning bush, Daniel and the fourth man in the fire, Isaiah in the temple, Paul on the road to Damascus. In modern times the near-death experience, reported by 5% of the population, describes what contemporary people believe is a personal encounter with God. Cardiologist, Dr. Pim van Lommel describes this experience in the following words, "The light is described as an extremely bright, non-blinding light that permeates everything. People are ineluctably drawn to this light and are completely enveloped by it. Sometimes this light is experienced as a being ... People always report direct communication with this being, as if it reads their mind and responds through the mind. While enveloped by this light, people experience total acceptance and unconditional love and have access to a deep knowledge and wisdom."[56] "Call to me and I will answer you, and will tell you great and hidden things that you have not known." (Jeremiah 33:3 NRSV).

Discussion Questions:

1. What is your understanding of the God of the Bible?
2. How have you experienced God in your life?

Memory Verse:

"Call to me and I will answer you, and will tell you great and hidden things that you have not known." (Jeremiah 33:3 NRSV).

What the Bible Says About Jesus - TLC Lesson 41

When I was a young pastor and a candidate for ordained ministry, I had to appear before a group of ordained pastors to be examined for ordination. They were permitted to ask any question they wished. I was nervous wondering, "What will they ask?" Suddenly one of the group blurted out, "Who is Jesus?" This was a fair question, one that all Christians must ask themselves. There are many answers to this question. The Bible says, "But there are also many other things that Jesus did; if every one of them were written down, I suppose that the world itself could not contain the books that would be written." (John 21:25 NRSV). It is my goal to share in a one page summary, "What the Bible says about Jesus." This, of course, must necessarily be a brief summary of the most vital teachings about him.

Chapter Six Understanding Scripture

1). <u>The Pre-existence of Christ</u>. Classical theologians assert that Christ was existent before the incarnation, one with God the Father (doctrine of the Trinity) and fully active in the creation of all things. "In the beginning was the Word, and the Word was with God, and the Word was God. He was in the beginning with God. All things came into being through him, and without him not one thing came into being. And the Word became flesh and lived among us, and we have seen his glory, the glory as of a father's only son." (John 1:1-3, 14 NRSV). "So now, Father, glorify me in your own presence with the glory that I had in your presence before the world existed." (John 17:5 NRSV).

2). <u>The Incarnation of Christ</u>. <u>Jesus</u>, the preexistent divine "Word" and the second person of the <u>Trinity</u>, "<u>God the Son</u>" was made flesh and conceived in the womb of <u>Mary</u>. The doctrine of the Incarnation, then, teaches that Jesus Christ is fully God and fully human, his two natures joined in one person. "And the Word became flesh and lived among us, and we have seen his glory, the glory as of a father's only son." (John 1:14 NRSV).

3). <u>The Atonement of Christ</u>. Human beings are reconciled to <u>God</u> through Christ's sacrificial death. Atonement refers to the forgiving or pardoning of <u>sin</u> through the death and <u>resurrection of Jesus</u> enabling reconciliation between <u>God</u> and <u>God's creation</u>. "For God so loved the world that he gave his only Son, so that everyone who believes in him may not perish but may have eternal life." (John 3:16 NRSV). "For if while we were enemies, we were reconciled to God through the death of his Son, much more surely, having been reconciled, will we be saved by his life." (Romans 5:10 NRSV). "And he died for all, so that those who live might live no longer for themselves, but for him who died and was raised for them." (2 Corinthians 5:15 NRSV)

4). <u>The Resurrection of Christ</u>. The resurrection of Christ from the dead is the central belief of the Christian faith. The resurrection is unique among all religions. The celebration of Easter is the high point of the Christian year. "For I handed on to you as of first importance what I in turn had received: that Christ died for our sins in accordance with the scriptures, and that he was buried, and that he was raised on the third day in accordance with the scriptures." (1 Corinthians 15:3-4 NRSV). "And if Christ has not been raised, then our proclamation has been in vain and your faith has been in vain." (1 Corinthians 15:14 NRSV).

5).The Second Coming of Christ. The Apostles Creed says, **"I** believe in Jesus Christ, God's only Son, our Lord, who was conceived by the Holy Spirit, born of the Virgin Mary, suffered under Pontius Pilate, was crucified, died, and was buried; he descended to the dead. On the third day he rose again; he ascended into heaven, he is seated at the right hand of the Father, and <u>he will</u> <u>come</u> to judge the living and the dead."[57] "They said, "Men of Galilee, why do you stand looking up toward heaven? This Jesus, who has been taken up from you into heaven, will come in the same way as you saw him go into heaven." (Acts 1:11 NRSV) "For as often as you eat this bread and drink the cup, you proclaim the Lord's death until he comes." (1 Corinthians 11:26 NRSV).

6). All the Rest! Detailed studies have been and can be done on all the topics above. For further information do an online search for, "theories of atonement", "views concerning the Second coming of Christ", "the pre-existence of Christ", etc. Further studies can be done on "the parables of Christ", "the miracles of Christ", and "the life of Christ".

Discussion Questions:

1. How would you answer the question, "who is Jesus?"
2. How have you experienced Jesus?

Memory Verse:

"But to all who received him, who believed in his name, he gave power to become children of God." (John 1:12   NRSV).

What the Bible Says About the Holy Spirit - TLC Lesson 42

The Holy Spirit is the third person of the Trinity who came to reside within Christ's disciples after Jesus rose from the dead. Jesus said to his disciples, "And I will ask the Father, and he will give you another Advocate, to be with you forever. This is the Spirit of truth, whom the world cannot receive, because it neither sees him nor knows him. You know him, because he abides with you, and he will be in you." (John 14:16-17 NRSV).

The Holy Spirit is not a vague impersonal force. He is a person equal in every way with God the Father and God the Son. He is considered to be the third member of the Trinity. The scripture known as the "Great Commission" makes reference to the trinity in these words, "And Jesus came and said to them, "All authority in heaven and on earth has been given to me. Go therefore and make disciples of all nations, baptizing them in the name of the Father and of the Son and of the Holy Spirit, and teaching them to obey everything that I have commanded you. And remember, I am with you always, to the end of the age. (Matthew 28:18-20 NRSV).

In TLC lessons 40 and 41 we talked about the attributes of God the Father and God the Son, Jesus Christ. Everything we said about the Father and the Son we can also say about the third person of the Trinity, the Holy Spirit.

Following are some attributes of the Holy Spirit:

1). The Holy Spirit is a Person. In the New Testament the Greek word for spirit (pneuma) is neuter, and yet in most places it is accompanied by masculine pronouns. For Example, "When the Advocate comes, whom I will send to you from the Father, the Spirit of truth who comes from the Father, **he** will testify on my behalf." (John 15:26 NRSV). "When the Spirit of truth comes, **he** will guide you into all the truth; for **he** will not speak on **his** own, but will speak whatever **he** hears, and **he** will declare to you the things that are to come. **He** will glorify me, because **he** will take what is mine and declare it to you." (John 16:13-14 NRSV).

2) The Holy Spirit Was Involved in Creation. "The earth was without form and void, and darkness was upon the face of the deep; and the Spirit of God was moving over the face of the waters." (Genesis 1:2 RSV).

3). The Holy Spirit is Involved in New Birth. "Jesus answered, "Very truly, I tell you, and no one can enter the kingdom of God without being born of water and Spirit. What is born of the flesh is flesh, and what is born of the Spirit is spirit. Do not be astonished that I said to you, 'You must be born from above. The wind blows where it chooses, and you hear the sound of it, but you do not know where it comes from or where it goes. So it is with everyone who is born of the Spirit." (John 3:5-8 NRSV).

4). <u>The Holy Spirit Brings Individuals to Repentance and Faith</u>. "And when he comes, he will prove the world wrong about sin and righteousness and judgment" (John 16:8 NRSV).

5). <u>The Holy Spirit Guides</u>. "For all who are led by the Spirit of God are children of God." (Romans 8:14 NRSV).

6). <u>The Holy Spirit Teaches and Reminds</u>. "But the Advocate, the Holy Spirit, whom the Father will send in my name, will teach you everything, and remind you of all that I have said to you." (John 14:26 NRSV).

7). <u>The Holy Spirit Comforts</u>. "I will not leave you comfortless: I will come to you." (John 14:26 KJV).

<u>Discussion Questions</u>:

1. How have you experienced The Holy Spirit in your life?
2. Do you ever pray to the Holy Spirit? Why?

<u>Memory Verse:</u>

"I will not leave you comfortless: I will come to you." (John 14:26 KJV).

What the Bible Says About Salvation - TLC Lesson 43

According to Christian belief, salvation from sin in general and original sin in particular is made possible by the life, death, and resurrection of Jesus, which in the context of salvation is referred to as the "atonement". The overwhelming majority agrees that Christian salvation is made possible by the work of Jesus Christ, the Son of God, dying on the cross.[58] I remember as a youth hearing for the first time what was told to me by a Christian friend about "God's Plan of Salvation." As I look back on that time, the

Chapter Six Understanding Scripture

content of what my friend shared seems so basic. It was not a discourse in deep theological terminology, but a simple summary of what the Bible is all about in a nut shell. While there is a lifetime of growth in understanding that brings the individual believer to a mature faith, the initial steps are as clear and simple as that first "plan of salvation I heard years ago! Please let me share it with you now.

1). <u>Human Beings Where Created to Live Eternally in Fellowship With God Free From Sin.</u> "Then the Lord God formed man from the dust of the ground, and breathed into his nostrils the breath of life; and the man became a living being." (Genesis 2:7 NRSV).

2). <u>Humans Sinned and Brought Upon Themselves Eternal Death and Original Sin.</u> "Then the Lord God said, "See, the man has become like one of us, knowing good and evil; and now, he might reach out his hand and take also from the tree of life, and eat, and live forever, therefore the Lord God sent him forth from the garden of Eden, to till the ground from which he was taken. He drove out the man; and at the east of the Garden of Eden he placed the cherubim, and a sword flaming and turning to guard the way to the tree of life." (Genesis 3:22-24 NRSV).

3). <u>God Came into The World Through Jesus Christ to Save Human Kind from Sin and Return Them To Eternal Life.</u> "For God so loved the world that he gave his only Son, so that everyone who believes in him may not perish but may have eternal life." (John 3:16 NRSV).

4). <u>Human Beings Must Acknowledge Their Sinful Nature.</u> "For all have sinned, and come short of the glory of God" (Romans 3:23 KJV). "Therefore, just as sin came into the world through one man, and death came through sin, and so death spread to all because all have sinned." (Romans 5:12 NRSV).

5). <u>Human Beings Must Confess Their Sin.</u> "If we confess our sins, he who is faithful and just will forgive us our sins and cleanse us from all unrighteousness." (1John 1:9 NRSV).

6). <u>Human Beings Must Accept Jesus Christ as Savior</u>. "For, "Everyone who calls on the name of the Lord shall be saved. (Romans 10:13 NRSV). "If you confess with your lips that Jesus is Lord and believe in your heart that God raised him from the dead, you will be saved." (Romans 10:9 NRSV).

7). <u>Those Who Confess Their Sin and Receive Christ Are Born Again</u>. "Jesus answered, Verily, verily; I say unto thee, except a man is born of water and of the Spirit, he cannot enter into the kingdom of God. That which is born of the flesh is flesh; and that which is born of the Spirit is spirit. Marvel not that I said unto thee, ye must be born again" (John 3:5-7 KJV). "So if anyone is in Christ, there is a new creation: everything old has passed away; see, everything has become new!" (2 Corinthians 5:17 NRSV). "For by grace you have been saved through faith, and this is not your own doing; it is the gift of God, not the result of works, so that no one may boast." (Ephesians 2:8-9 NRSV).

8). <u>The Saved Are Called to A New Life</u>. "Do your best to present yourself to God as one approved by him, a worker who has no need to be ashamed, rightly explaining the word of truth." (2 Timothy 2;15 NRSV).

9). <u>The Saved Are Destined to Live The Eternal Life Intended by God From The Beginning</u>. And I saw the holy city, the New Jerusalem, coming down out of heaven from God, prepared as a bride adorned for her husband. And I heard a loud voice from the throne saying, "See, the home of God is among mortals. He will dwell with them; they will be his peoples, and God himself will be with them; he will wipe every tear from their eyes. Death will be no more; mourning and crying and pain will be no more, for the first things have passed away." (Revelation 21:2-4 NRSV).

<u>Discussion Questions</u>:

1. How and when did you experience salvation?
2. What has happened in your life since you were saved?

<u>Memory Verse</u>:

Chapter Six Understanding Scripture

"For, "Everyone who calls on the name of the Lord shall be saved. (Romans 10:13 NRSV).

~Chapter Seven
Becoming a TLC leader ~

The Counter-Intuitive Nature of TLC Groups

The 59 minute meeting.
No food.
Multiply the groups annually.
Learn to pray out loud.
Learn to witness more effectively.
Growth in giving.
Worship weekly rather than monthly.
Apply spiritual gifts via personal and group mission.

The Role of Hosts

1. Provide a meeting place for a TLC Group. (Home, church, restaurant, or business place).
2. Arrange chairs in cooperation with the TLC Pastor (Leader).

3. Meet people at the door and show them where to put coats, etc.

4. Set the atmosphere of love and acceptance for regular attendees and guests, by calling them by first names and by introducing them to others.
5. Coordinate a simple refreshment time once every six weeks or so following the meeting, but not weekly. Let the group decide on this.
6. Be committed to the vision and mission of your local church and be loyal to its leadership and Staff.
7. Remember to keep the 59 minute rule!

The Role of TLC Pastors

1. Lead a TLC group in cooperation with a TLC Host.

2 Be committed to living the Christian life style and pray daily for the success of Christ's ministry through your local church.

3. Be committed to the vision and mission of your local church and be loyal to its leadership and Staff.

TLC Groups for Busy Disciples

4. Complete the TLC Pastor training.

5. Keep a record of TLC attendance an turn in the report once per month to the small group's pastor.
6. Contact inactive TLC members by telephone or email and encourage them to attend.
7. Remember to keep the 59 minute rule!

8. Recruit a TLC Pastor Apprentice and a Host and Backup Host apprentice as a part of your TLC group and train them for leadership through the group.
9. Provide child care vouchers for parents and turn into church office once per month.
10. Encourage your group members to attend worship and Sunday school on Sunday morning.

How to Recruit Lay Pastors and Hosts

1. Pray at the beginning and all the way through the process.
2. Make a list of potential persons from the church directory or other sources.
3. Call ahead and arrange a sit down meeting.
4. Use the TLC book to explain their role.
5. Focus on the graphic in the front of the book.
6. Briefly describe the curriculum.
7. Review "The Order of a TLC Meeting" section and tell about the 59 minute rule.
8. Read over the "Role of Hosts", or "Role of TLC Pastors", depending on who you are recruiting.
9. Ask if there are any questions.
10. Ask for a commitment. "Will you be a TLC Pastor/Host?"
11. Set a deadline.
   If they ask, "When do you want to know?" answer right now!
   If they ask, "how long do I have to get back to you?" answer two days?
12. If they do not call back in two days, you call them.

The Critical Components

Chapter Seven Becoming a TLC Leader

The TLC experience can only be successful if certain key elements are present in the process. Like so many other life endeavors there are some things without which the adventure will not succeed. The following are several such critical components.

1). Pastoral leadership. It is my deepest conviction that the TLC process can only succeed in a local church if the senior, or lead pastor, is fully committed to the idea. The pastor must not only be committed to the idea but must be the driving force behind this vision. The pastor must be actively recruiting leaders. The pastor must him or herself be leading a group as a TLC pastor. As the TLC process takes effect the spiritual DNA of the congregation will change. This DNA must be constantly reinforced. Only the lead pastor accompanied by a core of dedicated laity can maintain and spread this DNA. I believe it will take 3 to 5 years for significant growth to take place. Consequently the lead pastor must be prepared for a longer pastorate. I truly believe that any church, even a small church, can see significant growth if the TLC DNA is strictly embedded in the heart of the congregation and followed religiously. For example, a church with 100 in worship can see a TLC group participation of 100 people within two years. By year three that same church can see a TLC group participation of nearly 500 and continue to grow from there. This then could be this start of a major church development. If the pastor stays with his congregation for 15 or more years the results will be amazing.

2). Paid staff leadership is critical. Associate pastors, Christian education directors, youth pastors, music staff, and all program staff should be required by the lead pastor, via their job descriptions, to be TLC pastors and lead a group. The paid staff will thus form a core unity that will reinforce the TLC DNA.

3). Prayer is essential. Every TLC pastor, host, and group member must maintain a FRAngelism list. Experience has shown that many TLC members fail to maintain this list and pray for nonmembers consistently. This is the key pivot point for the whole endeavor. This is the critical part of the DNA which must be learned and constantly reinforced. Each TLC group member must be prepared to constantly pray for 20 or more people and be ready to bring one new member into their group each year. In this part of the process breaks down the groups and the church will fail to agree!

TLC Groups for Busy Disciples

4).The Essential Accomplishment. The end result of prayer, leadership, and DNA reinforcement must be the successful invitation of new people to the groups and eventually to Sunday morning worship. In my opinion, the major cause of worship decline in many American churches is the failure of its members to successfully bring new people on board. In the end this depends on the process of personal evangelism which every Christian is called to do effectively. A review of the TLC lesson entitled, "The Ultimate Walk across the Room", will help to reinforce this conviction.

5). Other Components for Success. Small group ministry, in my opinion, is only one of a dozen or so components necessary for spiritual success and growth in the local church. The total ministry context must be taken into consideration. Here is a brief listing of some of those components. In order for a church to grow, the leaders must pay attention to the following:

A). Conflict Freedom. If there is any major conflict with the church this must be addressed first and immediately before growth can happen.

B). Pastoral Leadership. There is a need for a visionary, risk taking, entrepreneurial lead pastor. The longer the tenure the better.

C). Staffing for Growth. There is a need to staff the church with paid servants and/or volunteers in the areas of children's ministry, youth ministry, music ministry, and office support staff.

D). Worship Opportunities. A variety of worship styles is necessary to meet the needs of the various generations of those in the ministry area of the church.

E). Adequate Facilities. Space is needed for ministry and programming either on site or off site.

F). Clear Mission, Vision, and Core Values agreement accompanied by specific goals. Be ready to plan your work and work your plan!

Chapter Seven Becoming a TLC Leader

G). Adequate Parking. Pay attention to the formulas for the number of parking spaces needed to match the sanctuary seating capacity.

H). Dynamic Biblical Preaching. Preaching that is not too long or too short. Preaching that combines Biblical insight with down to earth illustrations, humor, insight and relevant topics.

I). Personal Contact with the Congregation. Pastoral visitation by the lead pastor and/or visitation pastor and/or trained lay visitors.

J). Dynamic Sunday School Classes. A strong nursery program plus children, youth and adult classes.

K). A Highly Functional Committee and Program Structure. An organizational structure that is well organized, permission giving and effective verses efficient.

L). A Clear Understanding of Church Size. Studies show that most churches do not understand their size. Leadership roles change with the size of the church. Without an awareness of the importance of size, pastors and congregations are doomed to failure.

In the 21st century American church scene the follow statistics are extremely important.

Ninety percent of churches have a worship attendance of 350 or less. Fifty nine percent of churches have a worship attendance of 100 or less.

It takes 150 worship attendees to support a fulltime ordained pastor, a part time secretary and a part time custodian.

Churches under 150 in worship attendance will continue to decline. Churches with over 350 in worship attendance may continue to grow.

All churches can grow if they seek to provide the "components for success" listed here plus a small group ministry life TLC Groups.

110

~ Chapter Eight – Supplements ~

Supplements

Spiritual Gifts Survey – Page 1
Rate each question by this scale: "This is like me"
0 = Not at all, 1 = Very Little, 2 = Little, 3 = Somewhat, 4 = Much, 5 = Very Much

Spiritual Gift No. 1

___ I am a very organized person.
___ I am a well disciplined person.
___ I like charts, lists, and reports.
___ I like to do detailed work.
___ I like everything in it's place.
___ I am not a procrastinator.
___ I like things done a certain way.
___ I am a task oriented person.
___ I keep my emotions hidden.
___ I like to follow directions.

___ Total score.

Spiritual Gift No. 2

___ I am very outgoing.
___ I often display enthusiasm.
___ I am tolerant of other peoples' weaknesses.
___ I am talkative.
___ I like to tell jokes.
___ I am comfortable talking about my faith.
___ I have a clear understanding of the Gospel.
___ I can be impulsive at times.
___ I am a people person.
___ I am not afraid to take risks.

___ Total score.

Spiritual Gift No. 3

___ I am usually enthusiastic.
___ I am a good listener.
___ I can motivate others to action.
___ I make decisions logically rather than emotionally.
___ I like to see others reach full potential.
___ I am results oriented.
___ I am a positive thinker.
___ I ask intuitive questions.
___ I like practical solutions to problems.
___ I like to talk with people one on one and in groups.

___ Total score.

Spiritual Gift No. 4

___ I really believe that God is active in our lives.
___ I find it easy to support others who have doubts.
___ I believe deeply in the power of prayer.
___ I am not discouraged by difficult situations.
___ I am an incurable optimist.
___ I believe in miracles .
___ I spend a lot of time praying.
___ I have a child like faith.
___ I seldom have doubts about my beliefs.
___ I am willing to take risks in supporting the church.

___ Total score.

Spiritual Gift No. 5

___ I am usually light hearted rather than depressed.
___ I am very aware of the needs of others.
___ I often keep to myself.
___ I am well organized.
___ I am always ready to give.
___ I have a strong interest in missions.
___ I am a very sympathetic person.
___ I am a generous person.
___ I am willing to sacrifice in order to give to others.
___ I trust the leaders of my church with finances.

___ Total score.

Spiritual Gift No. 6

___ I like to visit the sick.
___ I believe in the power of prayer.
___ I believe in miracles.
___ I am a very supportive person.
___ I am intuitive about the needs of people.
___ I like to strengthen relationships within the church.
___ I feel called to pray with others.
___ I believe that God can heal the body, spirit, and emotions.
___ I believe in the effectiveness of modern medicine.
___ I have a strong compassion for others.

___ Total score.

Spiritual Gift No. 7

___ I like to work with other people toward a goal.
___ I like to use my skills and talents to aid others.
___ I place a high priority on relationships.
___ I am thought of as a friend to others.
___ I feel that I have helped myself when I help others.
___ I like to lift up others sense of self esteem.
___ I quickly discern the needs of others.
___ I am a very sympathetic person.
___ I enjoy one on one ministry over large groups.
___ I believe God loves even the greatest sinner.

___ Total score.

Spiritual Gift No. 8

___ I like to organize information for projects.
___ I like to study the Bible and read other books.
___ I am a very analytical person.
___ I am able to understand complicated things.
___ I know how to give simple clear directions.
___ I am a very logical person.
___ I love to study and discuss difficult subjects.
___ I am often asked to explain things.
___ I often think and speak theologically.
___ I have a gift for understanding the Bible.

___ Total score.

TLC Groups for Busy Disciples

Rate each question by this scale: "This is like me"
0 = Not at all, 1 = Very Little, 2 = Little, 3 = Somewhat, 4 = Much, 5 = Very Much

Spiritual Gift No. 9

___ I can get people to work together toward a goal.
___ I am able to give directions to others.
___ I have a vision for the future.
___ I often accept responsibility for leadership.
___ I am not afraid to take risks.
___ I am able to make unpopular decisions.
___ I am able to work well with conflict.
___ I see leadership as different than management.
___ I have a strong sense of God's will in my life.
___ I dream big dreams for the future.

___ Total score.

Spiritual Gift No. 10

___ I am usually good natured.
___ I do not like to analyze details.
___ I am sympathetic and sensitive to others' needs.
___ I like to comfort people.
___ I seldom complain about anything.
___ I remember people's names and faces.
___ I identify emotionally with others.
___ I am a very forgiving person.
___ I empathize with hurting people.
___ I believe God has a plan for each life.

___ Total score.

Spiritual Gift No. 11

___ I am not very patient with people's problems.
___ I have a strong sense of duty.
___ I do not worry about what others think.
___ I am usually not inhibited and am expressive.
___ I am seldom indecisive.
___ I can discern and share Biblical truths.
___ I believe that change is a natural part of growth.
___ I am able to confront people with the truth.
___ I do not feel the need to be popular.
___ I believe that God has a plan for every person.

___ Total score.

Spiritual Gift No. 12

___ I have a strong sense of loyalty to my local church.
___ I enjoy manual projects.
___ I am usually easy going.
___ I am a good listener.
___ I am a strong team player.
___ I would rather be on a committee than serve as leader.
___ I like to go on mission trips.
___ I am very supportive of the leader.
___ I feel called to lay ministry.
___ I stick to tasks until completed.

___ Total score.

Spiritual Gift No. 13

___ I am usually very patient.
___ I am a good listener.
___ I am a jack of all trades.
___ I often pray for others.
___ I love people.
___ I am seen as authoritative.
___ I am more a leader than a follower.
___ I am expressive, composed and sensitive.
___ I like to study.
___ I have a burden to see others learn and grow.

___ Total score.

Spiritual Gift No. 14

___ I love the Bible.
___ I like to read.
___ I like to work with groups of people.
___ I am usually technical and methodical.
___ I like charts, graphs and lists.
___ I have an organized system to store facts.
___ I like to do research.
___ I am always looking for ways to communicate better.
___ I ask a lot of questions.
___ I am an objective thinker and look for the facts.

___ Total score.

Spiritual Gift No. 15

___ I like to make practical applications of Biblical truths.
___ I am not afraid of complex or paradoxical situations.
___ I am often asked for advice.
___ I am known for my depth of understanding.
___ I am able to find simple solutions to complex problems.
___ I am able to cut through to the essence of an issue.
___ I am known as a practical person.
___ I am not embarrassed to offer simple answers.
___ I see God as active in all things and in all people.
___ I am interested in a wide range of topics and ministries.

___ Total score.

Please list the scores of your top five gifts here and on pages 3 to 7 and on page 8 in the box.

_____ Highest
_____ Next
_____ Next
_____ Next
_____ Next

Supplements

Spiritual Gifts Defined in Alphabetical Order

_____ Spiritual Gift # 1 <u>Administration</u>: Administration is the ability to organize information, events, or material to work efficiently for the body of Christ. The administrator can see a local church's ministries in full scope, past present and future. He or she likes to work with a plan. Administrators usually are well-organized, disciplined, and like everything in its place. They tend to be task oriented and hard-working. He or she likes to do detailed work and seldom procrastinates. Administrators are good with charts, lists, and reports. Administrators are like managers and focus predominantly on organization, details, schedules and skills instead of on the relationships and people involved. Administrators are sometimes confused with leaders. Leaders however work more with relationships, vision, risk-taking and overall planning. Leaders work to put a plan in place. Administrators work to keep the plan working well. The word for administrator appears only one time in the New Testament in 1 Corinthians 12:28. The word as used outside of Scripture refers to the helmsman who steers a ship to its destination. This suggests that the spiritual gift of administration is the ability to steer a church toward the fulfillment of its goals by managing its affairs and implementing its necessary plans. Administrators must be admonished not to over emphasize efficiency to the neglect of effectiveness. Efficiency is doing things right and effectiveness is doing the right things. Leaders help the church to do the right things while administrators work with making things efficient.

_____ Spiritual Gift # 2 <u>Evangelism</u>: Evangelism is the ability to be unusually effective in leading unbelievers to a saving knowledge of Christ. Evangelism comes from the Greek word meaning to announce or proclaim the good news. People with this gift are good at making new disciples. People with this gift are usually very outgoing, enthusiastic, good listeners, and comfortable talking about their personal faith. They frequently

TLC Groups for Busy Disciples

think about the unchurched and maintain very detailed FRANgelsim list. They have a solid knowledge of the Bible and are very good at learning memory verses. They can quote key Scriptures with ease. Every Christian is called to share their faith and to do evangelism, but the person with the gift of evangelism has an extraordinary ability to share faith and to win others to faith. They are unusually comfortable in talking with people, and people are very comfortable with them. They tend to make friends with the secular culture and are respected for their beliefs. They are very aware of the special needs of individuals and are able to discern and share how the gospel can meet those needs. The gift of evangelism is mentioned in Ephesians 4:11.

_____ Spiritual Gift # 3 <u>Exhortation</u>: Exhortation is the gift of motivating others to respond to Christian faith by providing timely words of counsel, encouragement, and consolation. This gift includes acts of standing by, sitting with, guiding, strengthening, inspiring, consoling, and comforting others. People with this gift stand ready to give an encouraging word, a needed hug, a listening ear, or a needed insight. Extorters have a deep intuition about the needs of others and are able to bring needed instruction, motivation, and direction at the exact moment it is needed. The biblical word for exhortation is close to the biblical word for comforter or Holy Spirit. The exhorter is able to come alongside other people in much the same way that Jesus promised that the Holy Spirit would come to our aid. The exhorter is usually very enthusiastic but humble. The exhorter is able to motivate others to action and likes to see people reach their full potential. The exhorter is a positive thinker and likes to talk with people one on one as well as in groups. The exhorter helps people to make decisions logically rather than impulsively, but is able to deal with emotional situations in a caring way. The gift of exhortation is mentioned in Romans 12

Supplements

_____   Spiritual Gift # 4 <u>Faith</u>: This is the ability to have a vision for what God wants to be done and to confidently believe that it will be accomplished in spite of circumstances and appearances to the contrary. The gift of faith transforms vision into reality. Every Christian has faith but the gift of faith is an extraordinary ability to believe and encourage belief in others in the face of challenging and difficult circumstances. One can easily see how this gift might relate to the gifts of exhortation and healing. A person with this gift helps others within the body of Christ to believe that all things are possible with God. People with this gift have a childlike faith and are able to accept something without questioning. They may speak of God's will in the face of certain issues, events, and projects within the church. People of faith are strong prayer warriors. People with the faith gift are able to support others who have doubts. They believe deeply in the power of prayer and are not discouraged easily. They believe in miracles and are incurable optimists. They are willing to take risks in supporting the church because they believe God will see them through. This gift is mentioned in 1 Corinthians 12:9.

_____ Spiritual Gift # 5 <u>Giving</u>: The gift of giving is the ability to contribute material resources with generosity and cheerfulness for the benefit of others to the glory of God. Christians with this gift need not be wealthy. This gift, is sometimes translated "generosity" and means "to turn over", to give over", or "to share". All Christians are called to give but God gives certain people an extraordinary sense of others' needs and the power to do something about it. People with this gift tend to have very cheerful hearts and have an overwhelming desire to give abundantly. People with this gift like to give quietly and without acknowledgment. They are never stingy and share with no strings attached. They are usually lighthearted rather than depressed and have a strong interest in missions. They are very sympathetic people. They are willing to sacrifice in order to give to others. They are generally willing to trust the leaders of their church with finances. In many cases these people are not wealthy but they give beyond reasonable limits. The gift of giving is mentioned in Romans 12:8.

_____ Spiritual Gift #6 <u>Healing</u>: Healing is the ability to call on God for the curing of illnesses, relationships, emotions, attitudes, and wounded souls. Inner healing, or healing of memories is also associated with this gift. People with this gift believe in the power of prayer and in miracles. They tend to have an intuitive sense about the needs of people. They feel a calling to pray with people. People with this gift also believe in the effectiveness of modern medicine. They believe in the combined power of prayer, modern medicine, and the medical community. They are likely to encourage others to live healthy lives, to visit their doctors regularly, and to have faith in God. They usually have a strong compassion for others. They are careful not to abuse their gift by expecting God to heal every person in every circumstance. They are very sensitive to the fact that healing is God's work. They know that sometimes God uses human vehicles to help in the healing process. They also know that sometimes people are not healed. They know that the lack of healing does not mean that the sick person has sinned, but that God has something different in mind. They also believe strongly that death is the ultimate healing and that the resurrection is the ultimate act of God making all things whole. Healing is often mentioned in the Bible. The Gospels record many healing stories in the ministry of Jesus. The specific reference to a spiritual gift for healing is 1 Corinthians 12:9.

_____ Spiritual Gift # 7 <u>helps</u>: This gift comes from the Greek word that means, "To aid and assist another in need". It is mentioned only once in the New Testament and appears to be distinct from the gift of service. Some suggest that while the gift of service is more group oriented, the gift of helps is more people oriented. The gift is reciprocal in that the receiver does as much for the giver as the giver does to the receiver.

Supplements

Helpers center on the needs of another person or persons but service centers on the worship of God. People with this gift give from their skills, talents, and energy to help others who have an apparent need. People with this gift are very aware of the needs of others. They place a high priority on relationships. They are thought of as friends by others. They quickly discern the needs of others. They are very sympathetic. They enjoy one-on-one ministry over large groups. These people tend to notice and assist with practical tasks that need to be done. They feel a spiritual link to others through routine tasks. They would rather be responsible for a set of tasks than be involved in leadership. They prefer to work behind the scenes and often avoid public recognition. They enjoy working at odd jobs, often seen as needing tended to, but without being asked. Experience shows that many people in the local church have this gift. It is mentioned once only in 1 Corinthians 12:28.

_____ Spiritual Gift # 8 Knowledge: This gift is the ability to discover, analyze, and systematize truth for the benefit of others and for the advancement of God's kingdom. People with this gift enjoy studying the Bible and other books to gain information about spiritual things. They are very analytical. They are able to understand complicated things. They know how to give simple clear directions and they are very logical persons. Others often ask them to explain things. They often speak and think theologically. They seem to have a natural gift for understanding the Bible. People with this gift have an extraordinary ability to comprehend the eternal truths of scripture and relate them in practical ways for everyday life. This gift is not confined to university and theological school graduates. Some of the greatest insights may come from persons with no formal higher education. People with this gift know how to discern between cultural biases and biblical truths. They are helpful in keeping the local church on track with its spiritual DNA and its core values. They are often able to articulate complex ideas in simple words and phrases. If combined with the gift of helps and the gift of exhortation the gift of knowledge may be used to build others up. People with this gift must be careful to avoid being authoritative and dogmatic. The gift of knowledge is mentioned in 1 Corinthians 12:8.

_____ Spiritual Gift #9 Leadership: This gift is the ability to motivate, coordinate, and direct the efforts of others in doing God's work. People with this gift are able to get people to work together toward a goal. They have a vision for the future. They are able to give directions to others in a caring way that creates willing followers. They are not afraid to take risks. They are able to make unpopular decisions. They work well with conflict. They see leadership as different from management. Management, like administration, is the ability to organize information or material to work efficiently for the body of Christ. Leadership is the ability to coordinate the efforts of the body of Christ to achieve the goals outlined in the information. Leaders are more interested in effectiveness than efficiency. Good leaders look for a balance between management and vision. Sometimes leaders can get too far ahead of others in the local church. With good managers at their side, leaders are able to keep things organized as they move ahead. Leaders will be careful to not be held back by over management, nor to be confused by lack of organization. Good spiritual leaders are always aware of the need for team ministry. They often model their style after Ephesians 4:11, "equipping the saints for the work of ministry". By utilizing all the spiritual gifts of the people in the local church, leaders are able to move the body of Christ forward successfully. The biblical reference for leadership is Romans 12:8.

_____ Spiritual Gift # 10 Mercy: The gift of mercy is the ability to deeply empathize with others and to engage in compassionate acts on behalf of people who are suffering physical, mental, or emotional distress. Those with this gift manifest concern and show kindness toward people who are

Supplements

often overlooked. All Christians are called to have mercy, but some have an extraordinary gift that causes them to feel the discomfort of others. Mercy shores are quick to come to the aid of people in need. They are usually good-natured. They like to comfort people. They seldom complain about things. They remember people's names and faces. They identify emotionally with others. They are very forgiving. They believe God has a plan for each life. People with the gift of mercy empathize with hurting people. Mercy shores must protect themselves from being victimized or used by others. Versus yours can be so sensitive, that others will take advantage. Experience shows that this gift is very common in the local church. There seems to be many more mercy shores than leaders or managers within the church. The gift of mercy is mentioned in second Corinthians 5:19.

____ Spiritual Gift #11 Prophecy: The gift of prophecy is the ability to receive and proclaim a message from God. It is the ability to proclaim God's truth in a way relevant to current situations and to envision how God would will things to change. This could involve foretelling future events, though its primary purpose is forthtelling. One who prophesies speaks to people for their strengthening, encouragement, and consolation. The gift provides a word from God to a specific group. A prophet is able to spot the difference between cultural trends in biblical truths. The profit is able to confront people with the truth of the situation. The prophet has a strong sense of duty. The prophet does not worry about what others think. The prophet is usually not inhibited and is very expressive. The prophet believes that change is a natural part of growth. The prophet does not feel the need to be popular. The prophet believes that God has a plan for every person. The prophet is not very patient with people's problems. Prophecy in the contemporary church has much more to do with giving guidance to the body of Christ or two individuals than it does to foretelling the future. Prophecy is often associated with powerful preaching. Prophecy means making known or speaking out or announcing vital information necessary for spiritual living and development. The gift is mentioned in first Corinthians 12:10, 29 and Ephesians 4:11.

_____ Spiritual Gift # 12 <u>Service</u>: The gift of service comes from the Greek word meaning "deacon" and relates to special acts of servanthood. This gift, unlike the gift of helps, is worship centered whereas the gift of helps is person centered. People with this gift have a strong sense of loyalty to their local church. They enjoy manual tasks and are usually easy-going. They are good listeners and strong team players. They would rather be on a committee then serve as the leader. They feel called to lay ministry. They will stick to tasks until they are completed. They view their life work as a form of worship and live for the building up of their church. Persons with this gift may tend to get overly involved in their local church out of the pure joy they receive from serving. Leaders in the church should take care not to miss use the dedication of lay servants. People with this gift like to go on mission trips. They are very supportive of their leaders and stick to tasks until completed. This gift is closely related to the gift of helps but is more focused on the institution of the church and the organization of the church than on its individual members. This gift is mentioned in Romans 12:7

_____ Spiritual Gift # 13 <u>Shepherd</u>: This gift is the ability to guide and care for other Christians as they experience spiritual growth. This is also called pastor/shepherd and can relate to the call to become an ordained pastor. This gift also is seen in laypersons with shepherding skills. Not all shepherds are ordained. Many shepherds are dedicated laypersons. People with this gift are usually very patient. They are good listeners. They are a jack of all trades. They often pray for others. They love people. They are viewed as authoritative by others. They are more leaders than followers. They are expressive, composed, and sensitive. They like to study. They have a burden to see others learn and grow. They

Supplements

tend to think in terms of groups, teams, and task forces rather than individual personalities. They enjoy encouraging others to develop their faith. They enjoy nurturing and caring for a group of people over a long period of time. They like to see people form long-term, in-depth spiritual relationships. The biblical word for shepherd means to protect, oversee, manage, care for, or to feed. Shepherds have a strong concern for growth and maturity within the members of their church.

____ Spiritual Gift #14 Teacher: The spiritual gift of teaching is the ability to clearly explain and effectively apply the truth of God's word so that others will learn. This requires the capacity to accurately interpret Scripture, engage in necessary research, and organize the results in a way that is easily communicated. Teachers love to study the Bible. They listen to other teachers, and often think of alternative ways to present materials. When they teach others are motivated to learn more about the Bible and their faith. They like to relate God's truth to life in a way that helps people grow and develop. Teachers like to work with groups of people. They are usually technical and methodical. They like charts, graphs, and lists. They have an organized system to store facts. They like to do research. They ask a lot of questions. They are objective thinkers and look for the facts. Teaching comes from the Greek word which means to teach, to instruct, to clarify, to illuminate, or to simplify. Spiritual teaching is more than objective data, more than mere biblical material it is a communication of a subjective experience with the risen Lord. The gift of teaching is given for the building up of the body of Christ, not just the imparting of facts. The gift of teaching and referred to in 1 Corinthians 12:28, and Ephesians 4:11. This gift is also linked to the gift of shepherd and is expressed in the book of Ephesians as pastor/teacher

TLC Groups for Busy Disciples

_____ Spiritual Gift # 15 <u>Wisdom</u>: The gift of wisdom is the ability to apply the principles of the Word of God in a practical way to specific situations and to recommend the best course of action at the best time. The exercise of this gift skillfully distills insight and discernment into excellent advice. People with this gift show a wide range of intelligence about many subjects and ministries. These people are able to act, speak, write, or apply God's eternal truths to the concrete realities of daily living in ministering to others. People with this gift are not afraid of complex or paradoxical situations. They are often asked for advice. They are known for their depth of understanding. They are able to find simple solutions to complex problems. They are able to cut through to the essence of an issue. They are known as practical people. They are not embarrassed to offer simple answers. They see God as active in all things and in all people. They are interested in a wide range of topics and ministries. This gift is related to the gift of knowledge in the sense of application. Wisdom is more than simply knowing the facts, it is applying the facts appropriately to Christian living. This gift is mentioned in 1 Corinthians 12:8.

Opportunities For Ministry

Gift # 1 Administration
__ Computer/Sound Tech.
__ Office Help.
__ Folding Bulletins.
__ Committee Secretary.
__ Committee Chairperson.
__ Organizing Schedules.

Gift # 2 Evangelism
__ Personal Testimony.
__ Music ministry.
__ Liturgist.
__ Evangelism Committee.
__ Handing out FTS lunches.

Gift # 3 Exhortation
__ Prayer Ministry Team.
__ Welcome Station Host.
__ Door Greeter.
__ Usher.
__ TLC Host/Back-up Host.
__ Music Ministry.

Gift # 4 Faith
__ Prayer Ministry Team.
__ Church Council.
__ Vision Team.
__ Music Ministry.

Gift # 5 Giving
__ Stewardship Campaign.
__ Finance Committee.
__ Mission Projects.
__ Mission Trip Fundraising.

Gift # 6 Healing
__ Barnabas Minister.
__ Stephens Minister.
__ Prayer Ministry Team.
__ Drug Ministry.
__ AA Ministry.

Gift # 7 Helps
__ Trustees Committee.
__ Church Painter.
__ Lawn Care.
__ TLC Host or Backup Host.
__ Mission Trips.
__ Music Ministry.

Gift # 8 Knowledge
__ Vision Team.
__ Historical Committee.
__ Education Team.
__ Children.
__ Youth.
__ Adults.

Gift # 9 Leadership
__ Committee Chairperson.
__ Committee Member.
__ Mission Trip Organizer.
__ TLC Lay Pastor.
__ TLC Host or Backup Host.

Gift # 10 Mercy
__ Barnabas Minister.
__ Stephens Minister.
__ Prayer Ministry Team.
__ Nursery Helper.
__ Drug Ministry.
__ AA Ministry.

Gift # 11 Prophecy
__ Membership Committee.
__ Long Range Planning Com.
__ Vision Team.

Gift # 12 Service
__ Funeral Dinners.
__ Kitchen Volunteer.
__ Party Organizer.
__ Altar/Communion Prep.
__ Communion Server.
__ Usher.
__ Greeter.
__ Welcome Table Host.
__ TLC Host or Backup Host.
__ Scripture Reader.
__ Music Ministry.

Gift # 13 Shepherd
__ Nursing Home Worship.
__ Barnabas Minister.
__ Stephens Minister.
__ Liturgist.
__ Scripture Reader.
__ TLC Lay Pastor.
__ TLC Lay Host or Backup Host.

Gift # 14 Teaching
__ Sunday School Teacher.
__ Nursery.
__ Children.
__ Youth.
__ Adults.
__ TLC Lay Pastor.

Gift # 15 Wisdom
__ Vision Team.
__ SPRC.
__ Building Committee.
__ Trustees.

Name: _____ Telephone: _____
Address: _____ Email: _____
City: _____ State: _____

Ice Breakers

1. If you had a time machine that would work only once, what point in the future or in history would you visit?
2. If you could go anywhere in the world, where would you go?

3. If your house was burning down, what three objects would you try and save?
4. If you could talk to any one person now living, who would it be and why?
5. If you HAD to give up one of your senses (hearing, seeing, feeling, smelling, tasting) which would it be and why?
6. If you were an animal, what would you be and why?

7. Do you have a pet? If not, what sort of pet would you like?

8. Name a gift you will never forget?

9. Name one thing you really like about yourself.

10. What's your favorite thing to do in the summer?

If I Were a . . .

A fun get-to-know-you icebreaker game to encourage creativity for small groups, you begin this game by having participants sit in a circle. The leader asks each person to say what he or she would be and why if they were a: A piece of fruit, An historical figure, A household object, A cartoon character, A cat, A dog, A flower, A tree?

Best/Worst. Have each person share their best and worst moments from the previous week. Try to steer the group away from school items. This icebreaker is an easy one to use at first and gives you good feedback concerning their life at the moment. Some veteran groups do this several times a year... the answers become more honest as you go.

Supplements

Most Unique. Go around the room and have each person share something that makes them different from anyone in the group, like, "I've never left the state I was born in" or "I am one of ten kids."

Two Truths and a Lie. Have each person make three statements about themselves: two true statements and one lie. For example, "I've never broken a bone. I have five sisters. I was born in Yugoslavia." The group tries to guess which statement is the lie.

Get To Know You Questions.

What do you do for fun?

What would be your ideal vacation?

What is the most memorable activity you did with your family as a child?

What quality do you appreciate most in a friend?

If you knew you couldn't fail and money was no object, what would you like to do in the next five years?

Mission Ideas

The following are suggestions and not meant to be inclusive. TLC groups select their own mission projects during the course of the TLC year. The following is a list just to prime the pump. Groups choose their own mission ideas prayerfully as the Holy Spirit leads and needs in the surrounding community arise.

1. Support the Ronald McDonald House.
2. Parent's Night Out.
3. Birth Day Angels.
4. Divorce recovery group.
5. Drug addiction support group.
6. AA support group.
7. Christmas Caroling to shut-ins or nursing homes.
8. Volunteer at the local food and/or clothing bank.

TLC Groups for Busy Disciples

9. Volunteer to support the Youth Ministry Team.
10. Volunteer to support the Children's Ministry Team.
11. Shoe box ministry.
12. Provide back to school packets.
13. Totally free car wash.
14. Hospitality ministry at church. (At the doors and in the parking Lot).
15. College student move in day – provide pizza.
16. Christmas gift wrapping.
17. Shut-in visitation ministry.
18. Leaf raking.
19. Lawn mowing and hedge trimming.
20. Tutoring.
21. Party for new people moving into community.
22. Window Washing.
23. Snow shoveling.
24. Free weekly lunch or dinner for the community.
25. Snow removal for senior citizens.
26. Transportation ministry to and from church or store.
27. Provide child care for small group parents.
28. Block party.
29. Sponsor a cornhole tournament for the church youth group.
30. Home repair projects like painting, handicapped ramps, etc.

Child Care Voucher

Name: _____

TLC Group No._____

Date: _____   Amount Provided: _____

Date: _____   Amount Provided: _____

Date: _____   Amount Provided: _____

Date: _____   Amount Provided: _____

Date: _____   Amount Provided: _____

Monthly Total: _____

_____

TLC Pastor Signature

TLC Groups for Busy Disciples

Egypt Syndrome

The Egypt Syndrome refers to a spiritual imperfection. The Israelites were enslaved in Egypt. When they began the exodus, things didn't immediately work out the way they expected. They started complaining that it would have been better if they had stayed behind in Egypt. The known slavery began to look better to the Israelites than the unknown risk of the wilderness.

There is a modern day Egypt Syndrome that infects the faith of Christians in the face of spiritual growth. This is especially prevalent in small group ministries that insist on annual multiplication of the groups. The purpose of multiplication is to make room for new people by expanding the groups. When group size reaches 20 people the group is too large close fellowship. The group then multiplies in to two groups of ten or so. Every time a group reaches 20 people, they are encouraged to multiply for the sake of new people. The catch comes when group members say, "I don't want to leave my current friends in the group." When this happens growth stifles and the Egypt Syndrome sets in. Ultimately the group ministry dies and so does the church.

The Egypt Syndrome is very subtle and affects group members without them realizing that it is short circuiting their essential mission to reach new people. Group members say, "We just want to stay together, what is the harm in that?"

Those who fall prey to the Egypt Syndrome typically vocalize the following rationalizations.

1. We'd rather make bricks that risk freedom in a new place we know nothing about.
2. Staying in the present circumstance is safe, less risky, even if it involves slavery.
3. It is the know way, not unknown.

4. We always did it that way.

5. We want to stay together and not multiply or divide our group.

Supplements

6. Backward direction, not forward.

7. It appears innocent but lacks wisdom.

8. It is afraid of vision.

9. It enslaves self and others.

10. It does not reach the Promised Land.

11. It wants to stay in the same old place with the same people all the time.

12. It models destructive behavior without knowing it.

13. It is often understood as the (human thing) to do. (God's thing isn't understood or is too scary.)

TLC Groups for Busy Disciples

FRANgelism

Friends	Relatives
Associates	**Neighbors**

Supplements

TLC   Monthly   Report

TLC   Pastor
      _____

Appr _____

Host _____

Date _____

No.	Last Name	First Name	Dates					
1								
2								
3								
4								
5								
6								
7								
8								
9								
10								
11								
12								
13								
14								
15								
16								

TLC Groups for Busy Disciples

Notes

Introduction

1. Dr. Dale E. Galloway, How to Create a Successful Church with Lay Pastors and Cell Groups, Hope Foundation, 1986.
2. David Lowes Watson, "Covenant Discipleship; Christian Formation through Mutual Accountability, April 30, 2002, WIPF& STOCK PUBL
3. David Lowes Watson, "Covenant Discipleship; Christian Formation through Mutual Accountability, April 30, 2002, WIPF& STOCK PUBL

Chapter One Praying

4. Bio Written by Matt Kinnell for Asbury University.

5. Rosalind Rinker, "Prayer Conversing with God", Zondervan, (Grand Rapids, Michigan 1959), p.18.
6. Betty Eadie. "Embraced by The Light, Bantam Books, New York, NY, 1992
7. Adapted from "The Edge", by Carol Ferch-Johnson and Bruce Manners.
8. Adapted from the Webpage "All About God".

9. Adapted from Got Questions Ministries, an online ministry, 2016.
10. Adapted from the article by Jim Burns, "Do I Pray to Jesus or to God?" Ignite Your Faith Website, 2016.
11. Prayer to the Holy Spirit from A Book of Prayers © 1982, International Committee on English in the Liturgy, Inc. (ICEL).
12. From the book Prayer for Beginners by Ignatius Press).

Chapter Two Witnessing

13. The United Methodist Hymnal, The United Methodist Publishing House, 1989, p.48
14. Pastor Ronald Riffle, What Does it Mean To Witness For Christ?, Cutting Edge Ministries, Gordo, AL, 2015.

Notes

15. Bill Hybels, <u>Just Walk Across The Room</u>, 2006, Zondervan, p. 19

16. Bill Hybels, <u>Just Walk Across The Room</u>, 2006, Zondervan,

17. Wikipedia, July 26, 2015 and *The United Methodist Hymnal* (1989) "Prevenient Grace" section, hymns 337-360 (<u>ISBN 0-687-43134-4</u>)

18. Wikipedia, September 7, 2015.

19. Baker's Evangelical Dictionary of the Bible, Copyright 1996, by Walter A. Elwell, Grand Rapids Mich.

20. Adapted from the *Transferable Concept: How You Can Be Filled with the Holy Spirit*, by Dr. Bill Bright, co-founder of Campus Crusade for Christ. © Campus Crusade for Christ.

21. *"Distinctive Wesleyan Emphases (Page 2)". Archives.umc.org. 2006-11-06.*

22. Bill Hybels, "Just Walk Across the Room", Copyright, 2006, Zondervan, p.116. Used by permission.

23. Professor Robert Atkinson, University of Southern Maine.

24. Jeff Dixon, the Key to the Kingdom: Unlocking Walt Disney's Magic Kingdom, p. 15.

25. Bill Hybels, "Just Walk Across the Room", Copyright, 2006, Zondervan, pp. 120-123.

26. Chris Walker, Website, EvangelismCoach.org, 1391 NW St Lucie West Blvd #383, Port Saint Lucie FL 34986.

27. Webpage, Daily Thoughts & Ideas for the Weary Optimist by Brian Norris.

28. Sermon by Adam Hamilton, Love: God so Loved the World, Church of the Resurrection, Leawood Kansas, December 6, 2015.

Chapter Three Worshipping

29. Adapted from, "Theopedia", online webpage.

30. Don Williams, "The heart of Worship Files", p.25, Regal Books.

31. The United Methodist Hymnal, The United Methodist Publishing House, Nashville, Tennessee, 1989 pp. 57-152

TLC Groups for Busy Disciples

32. "Worship Habit: Stop Talking and Start Living A Lifestyle Of Worship," by David Santistevan, online article.
33. "The Heart of Worship Album", Matt Redman, 1999.

34. "Church Attendance Rises", by George W. Cornell, Associated Press, February 16, 1991.

35. Clarke, Adam. "Commentary on Hebrews 10:25". "The Adam Clarke Commentary", 1832.
36. Adapted from Dr. Bruce Humphrey, Sermon series on psalms.

37. Should Worship Be Fun? By Bob Kauflin on February 6, 2007 in Defining Terms, Worship and Life, Worship and Music.
38. Having Fun in Church, 2010 JUNE: Church, Fun, Joy, Pleasure by Julie Clawson.
39. Why should Christians go to church? How important is it? , By Dr. John Beeehtle, Christian Answers.net, quotation of Alan Stibbs, God's Church, p. 92.

Chapter Four Serving

40. Duffield and Van Cleave, *Foundations of Pentecostal Theology*, p. 334
41. Kenneth Cain Kinghorn, Gifts of The Spirit,© Abingdon press 1976 Used by Permission, pp.22-23.
42. Quoted from a Sermon by Rodney Buchanan, United Methodist Pastor, "Why Are We Here?"
43. "The Greening of the Church", by Findley B. Edge, ©Word Books 1971 Used by permission.

Chapter Five Giving

44. Right on the Money, by Brian K. Bauknight, ©Discipleship Resources, Nashville TN, 1993 Used by permission.
45. Ibid.
46. Ibid.
47. Ibid.
48. Ibid
49. The Disciple's Path, by James A. Harnish, © Abingdon Press, Nashville TN, 2012. Used by permission.

Notes

Chapter Six Understanding Scripture

50. Biblegateway.com: A searchable Bible in over 150
    versions.
51. The Navigators, PO Box 6000, Colorado Springs, CO 80934-
    6000, 719-598-1212.
52. Biblegateway.com

53. See Gerald Schroeder, Orthodox Jewish Physicist, "Believe in
    God in Five Minutes", You Tube, August 2, 2014.
54. Merriam-Webster Dictionary.

55. The Free Dictionary.

56. Dr. Pim van Lommel, M.D., "Consciousness Beyond Life The
    Science of the Near-Death Experience", Harper One, 2010,
    pages 33-34.
57. "Apostle's creed". Worship – Evangelical Lutheran Church in
    America. Renewing worship. Retrieved 2011-05-19.

58. "Christian Doctrines of Salvation.: Religion facts, June 20, 2009,
    http://www.religionfacts.com/beliefs/salvation.htm

Extra Notes

59. Dunn, Michael. *Quotes on faith* (9th September 2013).
    theoryofknowledge.net.

TLC Groups for Busy Disciples

Resources for Further Reading

Introduction

"20/20 Vision, How to Create a Successful Church with Lay Pastors And Cell Groups" by Dale E. Galloway.

Praying

"Prayer: Conversing With God" by Rosalind Rinker.

"Prayer: Does It Make Any Difference?" by Philip Yancey.

Witnessing

"Faith Sharing" by Eddie Fox.

"Just Walk Across The Room" by Bill Hybels.

"The Master Plan of Evangelism" by Robert Coleman.

Worshipping

"The Heart of Worship Files" by Matt Redman.

Serving

"Gifts of the Spirit" by Kenneth C. Kinghorn.

"The Path: Creating Your Mission Statement for Work and for Life" by Laurie Beth Jones

Giving

Resources for Further Reading

"Right on the Money: Messages for Spiritual Growth Through Giving" by Brian K Bauknight.

Understanding Scripture

"30 Days to Understanding the Bible" by Max Anders.

A Final Word

When I was 17 years old, back in the 1950s, I was a very poor student in high school with failing grades in several subjects. I feared I would not graduate with my class. Then in 1959 my life was transformed through a personal encounter with Jesus Christ facilitated by my local E.U.B. Church. Within weeks my grades went from failing to my being listed on the honor role. The rest is history. I became a pastor in what was to become the United Methodist Church. I have served Christ through the church since 1963. I have been a pastor, a district superintendent, a visitation pastor, and a small group pastor over the past 53 years. I am just as confident today as I was in 1959 that Jesus Christ can change lives. I have written this book with the sincere hope that it will help you to experience that same life-changing relationship with Jesus Christ and that it will help you to lead others to do the same. I pray that you may be successful through TLC groups in your ministry.

With the years I have left to serve the Lord, my dream is to spend time consulting with Pastors and local churches. I believe that every pastor and every local church has the potential to reach the world for Christ. I invite you to contact me for any help you feel I might give in your work for Christ.

A Vision and a Proposal

It is estimated that 59% of congregations in America have a worship attendance of 100 or less on Sunday morning. It is further estimated that 90% of American congregations have a Sunday

TLC Groups for Busy Disciples

morning worship attendance of 350 or less. Approximately 50% of all church attendees go to a church with 350 or more worshippers on Sunday morning. There are many small churches in America struggling for survival led by pastors and laity that are often discouraged. Please remember that every large church was once a small church! **And so I have a vision!** Imagine that a church with 50 people in attendance calls me up and says, "Help us grow."This is what I would do.

First make sure the critical components mentioned on pages 107 to 110 are in place. Then -

1). Ask everyone to pray, pray, pray!
2). Have the pastor volunteer to become a TLC Pastor.
3). Have the pastor recruit one other staff member or lay person to become a TLC pastor.
4). Have the pastor recruit two TLC Pastor Apprentices.
5). Have the pastor recruit two host families (individuals of couples).
6). Have the pastor recruit two backup host families (individuals or couples).
7). Invite Dale Turner to train this total group of about 12 people in the process of doing TLC groups.
8). Begin two TLC groups, one led by the pastor and another by the trained TLC pastor, including the hosts and backup hosts.
9). Grow the two groups to 20 people following this book very closely!!! (A total of 40 participants by the end of year one).
10). Begin year two with four groups of 10 people and grow them to 20 people each. (total participants of 80 by the end of year two).
11). Begin year three with eight groups of 10 people and grow them to 20 people each. (total participants of 160 by the end of year three).
12). Begin year four with 16 groups of 10 people and grow them to 20 people each. (total participants of 320 by the end of year four.
13). Begin year five with 32 groups. You now have a cell church that is growing exponentially!

You say, "Dale, is this impossible!?" I say, "With God all things are possible and this has been done many times before." **It is my belief that almost any church anywhere could do this. It**

Resources for Further Reading

is also my belief that every church everywhere is called to do this!

I am available to help your church do this. There is only one hitch. At my age and stage of ministry I am not able to do this with individual churches. I would be able to do this with six to ten or more churches at one time. I have a three hour training workshop prepared for any group of pastors and churches that might want to try this. There is a basic cost for consulting, workshop materials, and expenses that is very affordable. I encourage pastors to form a group of churches for a training experience. I can be contacted at:

dale6@roadrunner.com or 330-335-0162

TLC Groups for Busy Disciples

Endorsements

I've known Dale Turner for over 20 years. During this time I've never seen him do anything that isn't near perfection. Such is the case with Tender Loving Care Groups for Busy Disciples. A detailed and doable approach to small groups.

> Bill Easum
> President, Effective Church Group.

Born out of the passionate, pastoral desire to form all people into vibrant, mature Christian disciples who will impact their community and the world, Rev. Dale Turner has produced Tender Loving Care Groups for Busy Disciples. Dale's over 50 years of ministry and commitment to the Wesleyan model of small groups have combined to produce a helpful, practical resource that can help spiritually transform not only the lives of those who participate in TLC groups but the congregation to which they belong.

> Rev. Dr. Gary George, Assistant to the Bishop,
> East Ohio Conference of the United Methodist
> Church.

TLC Groups for Busy Disciples is an excellent primer of personal holiness. It is group based and family sensitive, a community that involves nurturing head, heart and soul.

> Bishop Jonathan D. Keeton, Illinois Great Rivers
> Conference of the United Methodist Church, retired.

I must admit the thought of becoming an apprentice TLC pastor seemed daunting, as did going to a complete stranger's home for the first time. Also I was not sure who else was going to be a part of the group, more unknowns. But the year has been a blessing. Our group has grown to know and care for each other, in spite of being varied in age and interest. Our common love of Christ and the easy study/discussion format has allowed for prayer, sharing, and spiritual growth with the extra blessing of developing true and lasting friendships. I look forward to a new year of sharing with new friends in Christ.

> Mrs. Merry Kostko, TLC Pastor, Wadsworth UMC.

Endorsements

One of the vital signs of Christian life is small circles of Christians who cling to one another for spiritual support and mutual accountability. Pastor Dale Turner has shared his experiential expertise in helping local churches to do this well in the Wesleyan way.

> Bishop Gregory V. Palmer
> Ohio West Area of the United Methodist Church.

Dale Turner has written a concise disciple-making "field manual" for busy Christians in the 21st century. It focuses on the basics of Christian discipleship in a simple, yet relevant format for both the mature and -most importantly- new believer. It can be used in any small group context with little or no preparation, and has the potential to renew and revitalize the small group ministry of any congregation. I recommend "Tender Loving Care Groups for Busy Disciples" to every pastor or church leader who struggles with leading busy disciples!

> Pastor Don Ebert
> Lead Pastor, Wadsworth U.M.C., Wadsworth, Ohio.

I was a bit apprehensive about joining a TLC group, as I am somewhat an introvert. I'm very pleased to have done so, having met some very nice folks in our group. We have gotten to know more about each other. Most importantly we are exploring our faith and get into some good, sometimes deep, conversations. This really helps us grow as Christians.

> Ms. Gerri Mollica
> TLC Group member